OUT TO LEAD

OUT TO LEAD

SHAPING QUEER LEADERSHIP

JONATHAN DROMGOOLE

NEW DEGREE PRESS

OUT TO LEAD

Shaping Queer Leadership

ISBN   978-1-63676-757-4   *Paperback*
         978-1-63676-758-1   *Kindle Ebook*
         978-1-63676-759-8   *Ebook*

Para ustedes;

My husband, Juan, who encouraged, supported, cooked, listened, read, reread, and dealt with me throughout this entire journey. He shared in the struggles as much as the successes.

To my biological family, John, Olga, Barbara & Brandon for their support—always;

To my Venezuelan family Karinna, Juan Carlos, & too many more to name;

To my friends R & Nick who continue to guide, listen, and support;

To our dogs Kenzo & Astrid for their unconditional love & patience.

To the children who hope & dream of one day being something more than what we're told we can be. To the beautiful & diverse LGBTQ+ community that I am so proud to call my own.

To the resilient leaders whose shoulders I stand on and those leaders still to come.

Se lo dedico,

Jonathan Dromgoole

Contents

___

Introduction

"IT'S YOUR TIME, ARE YOU READY?"

You have been getting ready for this moment your entire life. You know that after this moment you can't go back. You won't be able to bottle up the words as they flow out of your mouth and gracefully enter the ears of those around you. At least you're hoping it goes like that. After all, they've supported you before, why would today be any different? In the back of your head, however, you know that these words could just as easily sound like a plate shattering in a crowded restaurant—the kind that not only demands attention but a response. Regardless, there is no turning back. You're ready. It is your time to come out and step into the spotlight.

Leaders are emerging within the LGBTQ+ community at an unprecedented rate. Not because we are some sort of a novelty making our first appearance onto the scene, but because we are finally harnessing the power of our resilience. From our coming out stories, sense of community, and contributions made throughout history, we have been navigating a world that fails to embrace us and see us as equals. But we have been there every step of the way. They say Rome wasn't built in a day. Well, let me add that it surely wasn't built only by straight Romans. Every society has benefited from the contributions of the LGBTQ+ communities and their leaders. From these trailblazers to those in elected office, pioneering medical advancements, and driving cultural change, it is through stories of resilience that we are becoming the next generation of leaders who are *Out to Lead*!

Resilience is a powerful force, one that is difficult to recognize and even harder to manifest. Google will give you millions of results in under a second when you just type "resilience" into the all-knowing search engine. In the top ten results, you get a guide from the Mayo Clinic on how to "build skills to endure hardship" or "a roadmap for adapting to life-changing situations and emerging even stronger than before" from the American Psychological Association. Hardship—check. Life-changing situations—check. Adaptability—have you met a queer person? We will go from out and proud to quiet and suspicious faster than those Google search results.

It is the very resilience we possess, especially the younger generations, that has created a new wave of global leadership. Choosing to run for office and placing your life in the public eye is challenging regardless of whether you're running for class president or president of a country. The challenges of pursuing a life of public service are magnified when you're set to be the historical first member to represent the LGBTQ+ community. So, when Pete Buttigieg, an openly gay millennial Democrat, made his announcement on April 14th, 2019, that he would be seeking the office of President of the United States, the pressure was on. Not only would he potentially bring along an entire generation to the Oval Office, but the LGBTQ+ community too. Even though Mayor Pete did not advance to become President Pete, I wonder to what degree his queerness and coming out process helped develop his resilience.

There is a growing number of leaders coming out, no pun intended, of the LGBTQ+ community, especially in politics. Dubbed the Rainbow Wave (Giardina, 2020), the gut-wrenching, suspenseful, and cathartic US elections season of 2020 has put forth the queerest Congress in history with a total of eleven members of the LGBTQ+ Congressional Caucus (Flores, Gossett 2020). In 2020, more than one-hundred and sixty queer candidates won their elections across the country (Victory Fund, 2021). According to the Victory Institute's Out for America Map, which tracks LGBTQ+ elected officials, there are now close to one thousand out and proud elected officials at all levels of government in almost every state. Well, except Mississippi. Queer Mississippians call me and we can chat on how to fix this.

However, it can't be simply because these candidates are queer that they are winning their elections. Profound levels of discrimination, setbacks, and limitations are often expected when coming out of the closet. Everyone believes that being anything but straight means your life will be hard and that your queerness will be a limiting factor making it almost impossible to achieve your goals and dreams. Many would argue that it is precisely because Pete Buttigieg is a proud gay man that he did not secure the 2020 Democratic Nomination.

When I came out and simultaneously chose to "bring in" others along for the ride, I was met with a certain hesitation. Almost immediately, I lost "friends," but I guess they weren't ever really my friends, and was told, "I will pray for you." I was, however, fortunate enough to not face overt discrimination from my family and those who mattered most, and I acknowledge the immense privilege in this. Instead, they were afraid that being out would instantly make life harder for me. They feared that going public about my sexuality would close more doors than it would open. They were, luckily, very wrong.

I spent twenty-one years creating a persona: one that would be distracting enough for people to ignore the fact that I was very much gay. I wasn't doing this intentionally every single time, but at some point it became common. From pursuing the most academically rigorous path possible, and to not just joining but leading various extracurricular organizations, I tried to distract everyone, including myself. I wanted to control the spotlight and show the world what I wanted everyone to see. I hid that I was struggling to come to terms with my sexuality in an environment that wasn't welcoming.

Since 2015, I have lived as an out and proud gay Latino/x man and I can truly say, *it gets better.*

All the time I spent in the closet, the struggles I faced coming out to myself, and those I faced coming out to others time and time again have given me the resilience to excel at a pace surpassing that of my straight colleagues. Being LGBTQ+ is a tremendous gift and, frankly, an advantage. Starting at a young age, we are used to having to excel at everything to make sure the focus is on our achievements and not our sexuality, which society overwhelmingly sees as a flaw. Well, let me tell you, even diamonds have flaws and honey, they sparkle. They captivate and are the product of immense pressure and resilience. So, you know what, the LGBTQ+ community is nothing short of the crown jewels. Link us all together and we light up the world with how bright we sparkle and shine.

My gayness isn't what intimidates others or makes them uncomfortable around me. Actually, my sexyality seems to make people want to talk to me and share their stories. It's as if I am some sort of hairstylist who must work double-duty to fix your 3 AM decision to give yourself bangs while also answering the meaning of life, and all for the price of a 'quick trim'. What is intimidating, however, are the products of queer resilience—leadership, ambition, and grit. My identity and struggles as a gay man have everything to do with my professional successes.

Queer resilience and leadership are assets for employers, families, friends, and yes, even the nation. There is clear evidence of this throughout history and this points to future potential. First, we, the queers, must realize and harness our resilience and fully embrace ourselves. RuPaul said it best, "If you can't love yourself, how the hell are you gonna love somebody else?"

Being gay and coming out into a society that does not yet consider this normal, has instilled in me a tremendous level of resilience. Leadership skills are magnified and developed at an earlier stage in our queer lives than our heterosexual counterparts. These skills are polished and harnessed exactly because of who we are. We can empathize with marginalized individuals because we too have faced discrimination. Virginia Delegate Danica Roem summed it up nicely for me once when I had the incredible honor of meeting her. "It is because of, not despite, our identities that we succeed."

PART I

HISTORY OF QUEER RESILIENCE

1

We're Here, We're Queer!

———

Popularity has nothing to do with it—let's leave that for the elections and high school class president races. Leadership is about more than just being liked. Leadership is about more than just being in front of the camera and taking up the spotlight. True leadership is about believing in something bigger than yourself. It is about having a mission and purpose that gets you up in the morning despite knowing that your job isn't a nine to five. Leadership is about having a story—here is mine.

THE LONE STAR STATE

Often, I introduce myself as "Mexican made, Texas-raised, DC educated." Before you make assumptions that I grew up with cowboy boots and a ten-gallon hat, that's not the Texas to which I am referring. The closest I ever got to owning cowboy boots was when I was five or six and dressed up as Woody from *Toy Story* down to the boot that said "Andy." I grew up in Austin, Texas. Nope, not the Austin that just popped into your head with the tall skyscrapers and the tech companies. The Austin I grew up in embodied its motto "*Keep Austin Weird.*" It wasn't just a slogan or a countermovement to the big business and cookie-cutter prefabricated houses that now make up Austin. This Austin, the authentic version with its wear-what-you-want-do-what-you-want culture, wasn't popular or trendy. Far from it, actually. Austin was a leader, focused on environmental sustainability and local organically grown produce, before it was the cool or hip thing to do.

Despite not being born an Austinite, my family has called it home since 2000. I spent my formative, and most of my closeted years, in Austin. Over the course of those twelve years, from the first grade to my senior year of high school, I watched that city grow, flourish, and prosper into the great city it has become. In 2008, faced with what was back then the worst economic crisis since the Great Depression, Austin somehow managed to escape without visible damage. Unlike many other great cities of the South, Austin did not have the mass migration of people leaving for better jobs and opportunities in faraway places. Instead, not just people, but large-scale companies began coming to Austin to set up businesses, start families, and create a future.

When I left Austin for Georgetown University, people would ask "Oh, where are you from?" Shyly, I often responded, "Austin, Texas, the capital," knowing very well that even some of the most educated students in the country had no idea where Austin was and about its role as the capital of the Lone Star State. Often their response was, "Oh, I thought the capital was Houston or Dallas. I've never heard of Austin." In the truest Gemini fashion, I prepared my unsolicited Ted Talk about how Austin was, in fact, the capital not only of Texas but of Live Music and home to both the tech, film, and music festival South by Southwest and Austin City Limits, a live music festival originally meant to feature Texan talent.

By the time I was finishing up my bachelor's degree at Georgetown, Austin had become wildly popular. During four short years, the city had firmly cemented its place as one of the top ten cities that millennials wanted to work in. For many reasons, this wasn't what I wanted. For twelve long years, I had watched that city become what it had always been destined to be. I watched Austin be threatened, tried, and tested only to come out stronger and more resilient. Yet, during those same twelve years, I was stuck. Stuck, like a tire in the mud of one of the large pickup trucks that intimidated silver Mazda drivers like me in the high school parking lot. I remained stuck in the mud, unable to escape and become who I truly was.

For all of its great achievements and accomplishments, Austin represented and, in many ways, continues to represent my inability to lead. It's the personification of the metaphorical closet, regardless of how many years and how much distance I have put between myself and that place. Though the Texas heat could have helped bake in the rainbow colors I was so desperate to show like a kiln for one of those vases you spend an entire Saturday morning trying to paint to perfection at a paint and sip, the Texas heat instead managed to crack my otherwise tough exterior. Every time I return to Austin as an out and proud gay man with my husband, I seem to retreat to the closet the moment the wheels touch down on the hot tarmac of Austin-Bergstrom International Airport.

It took me a long time to realize that the proximity of Austin to Mexico is what dignified it as an international airport. Now, it has a broader range of flights. However, as a Mexican American who constantly traveled back and forth between both countries growing up, there seemed to be nothing international about the city. It was just another way of life to have to straddle the identity of both countries and cultures, to have the constant mix of Spanish and English in everyday speech. Being both Mexican and American was so normal to me growing up in Texas that it didn't seem to make one foreign or international. Yet, we had an international airport.

Regardless of how liberal Austin may have been and has continues to be, it is still only a small dot of blue in a sea of otherwise conservative values. Maybe it was the fact that Texas was once its own country—a fun fact taught to us in seventh-grade history class that only encouraged my Ted Talk tendencies—or the fact that Texas is the only state allowed to fly its flag at the same level as the US Flag (Texas House of Representatives, 2021). Maybe it is the fact that the Texas Capitol is taller than the US Capitol (Texas State Preservation Board, 2021). Perhaps it was the combination of all these facts that allowed Texas to intimidate me.

Instead of feeling that I am coming home to see my family, the feeling that constantly creeps in is that I am coming back to a place that never gave me an opportunity to be myself. A place where, for years, I had put my head down and focused on everything but my personal life. Even in Austin, with its "weird" vibes, I never felt like it had the right conditions for me to come out. You would think that the ultra-liberal city that almost elected Albert Leslie Cochran (Schwartz, 2012), a beloved homeless man who frequently paraded around Austin in nothing but a leopard thong and heels, as Mayor in 2003 would be the place for a "baby gay" to come out. However, for me, that just wasn't the case.

My Austin wasn't that Austin. My Austin was one where the broader conservative religious values of Texas were very much present. My Austin was one where white privilege was shoved in my face before I even understood what that meant. Instead of being weird, Austin was and continues to be white. It is a city that has cleverly separated communities of color to the East of I-35 and the wealthy Northwest of the river.

Austin is also where, from a young age, I was told and made to feel that I had no potential of succeeding and getting ahead because of my Latino heritage. Early on in elementary school, I was told directly by my teacher that I would not be allowed to go onto the next grade if the other Mexicans in the class didn't pass because we were all the same. Come to think of it now, I don't even think the other kids were Mexican. That same teacher once asked me how to say something in Spanish, my first language, but when I translated for her, she scolded me saying it was incorrect and that I shouldn't be speaking that language anyway. To this day I don't understand how a teacher, especially one who was herself Latina, would go out of her way to discourage children from reaching for more.

VIVA MACHISMO?

As much as a physical place can impact the development of leadership, a family can equally do the same. I had it easy. By no means is my family conservative or attached to a religion or political ideology. They are, however, Mexican. For any Mexican reading this, you know where this will go. You know how our culture and traditions are established on a foundation of homophobia and fragile masculinity that we cleverly disguise as *Machismo*. As if putting the word "macho" in it somehow magically hides the fact that it screams the opposite. Now, don't get me wrong, I love a good pozole or tacos de barbacoa as much as the next non-vegetarian Mexican, but growing up in a Mexican household in Central Texas, even a liberal one, does not make it easy to deviate from expectations.

My family didn't have to, nor did they, openly state any expectations of me. They simply asked that I finish high school and not leave a girl pregnant—two easy asks for a closeted gay kid. Expectations were always there though. Don't mess up, don't ruin or waste the sacrifices your family made to get to America, don't ask for money, and whatever you do in life, be that a teacher, elected official, office worker, or even a stripper, be the best at it. Make sure that you surpass and do better than your parents. This went hand in hand with 'don't disappoint your parents'—that one haunts me to this day.

Society, however, wanted more of me than just this. Every Mexican *telenovela* depicts Mexican men in essentially two ways. It's as if TV Azteca and Televisa had created their own version of Leonardo da Vinci's *Vitruvian Man* only, you know, Mexican. Mexican men are either the passionate, sexy, *Latin Lover* type with big muscles, or the passionate, sexy, *Latin Lover* type with big muscles who also happens to be dominant, abusive, and aggressive to those around them, especially women. Can we say *fragile masculinity* louder for those in the back?

Essentially if either Jaime Camil or Fernando Colunga have played them, then they likely fit, to some degree, these roles. Now there are also the Mexican men who are the stereotypical Narco, but these likely fall under one of the two already stated archetypes. Now you might be thinking, but Jonathan, what about the wise old man in Coco, he's Mexican and not *machista?* Don't worry young grasshoppers, I'm getting to Disney in a moment. Despite these "old wise men" characters, let's be honest with ourselves; they were likely one of the original incarnations of TV Azteca's and Televisa's *Mexican man.* While these two depictions of manhood established by the two largest TV networks in Mexico may have slight modifications, they never deviate from the literal straight and narrow path of being, well, straight.

LGBTQ+ characters in Mexican TV are not common and if they are included, then they don't play a central role in the narrative of the series. Due to this, queer characters aren't depicted as multifaceted individuals and are often simply boiled down to one characteristic—their sexuality. It is through the character's sexuality, in this limited and one-dimensional representation of queer characters in *telenovelas,* that their storylines are developed. This means that they tend to focus on the problems, as they see it, that come with being queer. Unfortunately, these characters are often bullied, made fun of, kicked out of their homes, or somehow get AIDS and die off-screen within one season.

Bullying, homelessness, and HIV/AIDS are all very real issues facing the LGBTQ+ community. We face higher levels of discrimination both within our homes and in society. Just take a look at the laws in the books around the world. According to the Trevor Project, the leading national organization providing crisis intervention and suicide prevention to LGBTQ+ youth, forty percent of the homeless youth population identifies as LGBTQ+. Then there is the HIV and AIDS pandemic, which does disproportionately impact the LGBTQ+ community (HRC). However, we must de-stigmatize and normalize the fact that AIDS is no longer a death sentence to members of the community. It is very possible to live a happy and healthy life, where the individual is undetectable and cannot transmit the virus thanks to advancements in medicine (HRC). Now, consider this; do you think we would be further along in the process of combating AIDS and HIV if the systems in place would have not originally called it the Gay-Related Immune Deficiency (HIV, 2021)? I certainly think so.

ALWAYS THE VILLAIN

Constantly seeing these narrow depictions of LGBTQ+ individuals in the daily Mexican media that dominated my upbringing was only reinforced by Disney. Looks like the queers weren't invited when both of my cultures simultaneously got together and said, "you know what, wouldn't it be great if we constantly showcased the LGBTQ+ characters in a negative light to deter people from being gay?" Just like *telenovelas,* Disney has historically exaggerated stereotypical qualities of LGBTQ+ individuals in their villains, never their heroes.

One of the more obvious representations is *The Little Mermaid's* Ursula, who was quite literally inspired by the famous drag queen Divine from *The Pink Flamingos,* from the makeup to the curves. However, Ursula also hides in the depths of the ocean, tricks people, and in the end, isn't accepted by the pretty mermaids and is killed. *Aladdin's* Jaffar depicts not just a power-hungry invisible character, but someone who is heavily drowned in feminine mannerisms. Jaffar is centered around tricking and deceiving people, especially other men like the Sultan, to like him and do what he wants. Governor Ratcliffe from *Pocahontas* also falls in line with Disney's heavy reliance on queer coding villains with his long flowy hair and pigtails with pink bows. Think about it - Hades from *Hercules,* Scar from *The Lion King,* or Gaston from *Beauty and the Beast,* they are all queer coded. The list goes on and on to include every single villain in the Disney universe in some way, shape, or form.

I didn't understand that what I was seeing in the media was homophobia, I just knew that there was blatant othering. There was the visible villainizing or caricaturing of certain effeminate characters on TV that I somehow, in the early stages of my coming out process, subconsciously connected with. At the same time, that connection and understanding meant that whatever was being reinforced as "wrong" or "incorrect" about them was also found in me. I always felt bad for these characters that were being made fun of or that somehow were cast in an evil light. I felt that there was so much more to them than just what we were seeing on the screen. So, you know that when a film about Maleficent's backstory was made, especially starring Angelina Jolie (#TeamJolie), I was all about it.

Even though these over-emphasized queer tropes have been firmly implanted and reinforced by the media, the Lesbian, Gay, Bisexual, Transgender, Queer, Questioning, Intersex, Asexual, Pansexual, Two-spirit + community is more than just our identities. We each have our own unique stories that add to the diversity of not just our queer community, but communities at large. To quote history-making Virginia General Assembly Delegate Danica Roem, it is "because of our identity and not despite it" that we succeed. Our sexuality and gender don't make up entirely who we are. Does being a straight, white, cisgender male define the entirety of a human that may fall into those categories? No, probably not. It may grant them a certain level of privilege, just like being LGBTQ+ makes us natural-born leaders.

The queer community has so many important stories to share. Mine is only one, and those throughout this book are not enough. We need more stories told by us and for us. For that, we need to know where we come from, how history has been shaped without us and even against us, how policy making for centuries was focused on exclusion rather than inclusion, and how (by force) it has taken us until the twenty-first century to lead. Now we are here, we are queer, and trust me, we aren't going anywhere.

2

Our history, or Lack of

Should I flood you now with a stream of inspirational quotes about the struggles faced by the LGBTQ+ community? Should I share with you just how difficult the LGBTQ+ community has it in every sphere, industry, or sector? Where would I begin, not just in terms of time and history, but the location in a world where even the most progressive nations still do not have adequate legislation for true equality? My community, the wonderful and diverse queer community with its multitude of intersectionalities, has an incredible history. It goes beyond what we are now just being shown in the media or the ballot box.

Before we were candidates for local and even national offices, before we were Academy Award or Grammy winners, and before any of the accolades and recognition we have recently begun to receive, we were ignored, ostracized, and imprisoned. Even before that, before we were considered the other, before our collective identities and being out and proud became illegal, we were just there. We have always been there.

It seems that there was a time when we existed, then suddenly we were gone from history, and now we are coming back. Add our historic vanishing act to the great mysteries of the world such as the disappearance of the Aztecs or what lies at the bottom of the ocean. Without needing to dust off a library card and plunge into stacks of history books, a quick Google search reveals a rather odd result. It appears that homosexuality was fine, accepted, and a common way of life from ancient times right until everything changed during the Middle Ages. Is it a coincidence that at the same time straight, white, European men—who likely benefited the most from the contributions of the queer community—decided that it was no longer *en vogue* to be queer, so they took the power of the pen and wrote our collective history out, putting us in the historical closet?

MY LITTLE QUEER LIBRARY

Nearly five-hundred years after the end of the Middle Ages, books by and for LGBTQ+ folks have begun to pop up in major bookstores. I remember the first time I found the LGBTQ+ book section as an independent, stand-alone part of the bookstore and not incorporated into the "self-help" section. It was tucked away and only had about three books, but it had its own little label. Since then, I have begun my own little bookshelf of queer theory and history books. This little, queer library represents how much our history was covered up over the ages. And while these are queer books, they are predominantly written by white, cisgender men rather than the queer individuals they are supposed to represent. This especially applies to the popular ones that garner media attention. Just like straight European men initially wrote the history of the world, very similar men have once again been given the privilege to dictate our story, therefore only representing but one tiny branch of our diverse community.

For many reasons, I've begun to look closely and critically at all the books on my shelf. Sorry not sorry J.K. Rowling, but off the shelves you go. Aside from sending J.K. Rowling to collect dust elsewhere, I have noticed that not only is it mainly white men who get to tell the stories of the LGBTQ+ community, but that our recent history seems to be only from the perspective of the United States. Yes, we have made tremendous strides in the United States towards increased equality, but we by no means have been a leader on this front.

Denmark was the first country to legalize same-sex unions in 1989, while the Netherlands became the first country to fully legalize same-sex marriage, effectively eliminating the difference between homosexual and heterosexual marriage in 2001 (Taylor, 2015). In fact, according to *Pew Research Center*, there was a country on every continent that had legalized same-sex marriage, except for Asia, by the time the Supreme Court of the United States made it the law of the land. Europe did it with the Netherlands in 2001, North America followed in 2005 with Canada, South Africa added Africa to the map with the passing of legislation in 2006, South America saw Argentina pass marriage equality in 2010 while three years later New Zealand did the same in 2013, bringing with it the Oceanic/Australian continent. Since 2017, same-sex marriage has been legal on the Asian continent through the passing of legislation in Taiwan, though restrictions and limitations in place limit full recognition of same-sex marriages (Masci, Sciupac, Lipka, 2019).

Yet, it seems that while America has not been the leader in the gay rights movement, it still dominates and controls the conversation. One of the many books on my shelf is the self-proclaimed "Limited Edition" of *Victory* by Linda Hirshman, which includes a handy chronology of the gay rights movements. Much like the conventional interpretation of LGBTQ+ history, the gay rights movement seems to have only started in the last one-hundred years or so. As if we haven't been fighting for our rights since Adam met Steve or that first cave-kid knew they just weren't like the other cave-kids in their nomadic tribe. Many of the highlights in the chronology showcase moments of defeat instead of triumph for our community, such as a "raid on gay bathhouse" in 1903, "New York State law demands 'orderly' bars" in 1934, or "the State Department announcing homosexual discharges" in 1950 (Hirshman, 2018).

Yes, there are some positive highlights, but they don't seem to appear until the late 1990s or early 2000s, by which point the timeline is essentially over. In defense of the book, it was originally published in 2012 before major achievements in the legislation were passed, such as marriage equality in 2015 ("Obergefell v. Hodges", 2015) and the recent anti-discrimination legislation of 2020 ("Bostock v. Clayton County", 2020). Even in the year that was 2020, the Supreme Court's decision was a little silver lining in a historic year.

Our history seems to be only seen through the lens of struggle, revolution, or fighting for our rights. It is in essence, and has always been, a history of resilience. We are a community that appears only in the context of when we have reached a critical mass or level of discrimination that forces us to come out of the closet and into the streets to demand justice. Moments in time, like the 1969 Stonewall Riots (PBS, 2020) or the 1987 National March on Washington for Gay and Lesbian Rights (Williams, 1987), were moments when our community in the United States said, "enough is enough." These moments have become well documented in the recent American context, but what about on a global stage?

THE POWER OF THE PEN

Many parts of the world have seen the development of an LGBTQ+ rights movement, even if it happens to be underground rather than mainstream. Even in countries where the punishment for homosexuality is the death penalty, the fight for equality is present. It may happen through online forums and blogs, where the seeds of equality can be planted without risking the identity, and life, of the advocate. Globally, the conversation and advocacy for Gay rights has been through the perspective and history of the West. Broadly speaking, and by looking at the laws on the books, many countries in Africa and Asia still criminalize homosexuality (BBC, 2021). In communities such as these, there are still cultural norms reinforced through historical gender roles, religious values, and political ideology that need to be overcome. There are many hearts and minds that need to be won before a discussion of LGBTQ+ rights can be front and center. Much like a cake needs the right ingredients, and then needs to be mixed and cooked at the right temperature, LGBTQ+ rights need the right cultural norms to come into question by enough hearts and minds, at the right political moment, for progress to be made. This is the way lasting change can be achieved.

Change requires the presence of the queer community in the broader public. These need to be brave LGBTQ+ individuals who, combined with critical allies, are ready and willing to change the hearts and minds of the whole. LGBTQ+ individuals must be present in the community or country where change is so desperately needed. Otherwise, it's easy to deny their existence. Every country and every city around the world has Lesbian, Gay, Bisexual, Transgender, and Queer people living in them at this very moment; even countries that claim they don't have gay people living in them. Some may be living out and proud, some may be living under the fear of prosecution, and some may be living without the understanding that they are part of a larger community.

Where in the world do we hear of a bright and vibrant rural gay community? Now, I'm not talking about a destination or place where the community comes together for less than a month out of the year, but a true place that we can call home away from home. Due to bullying, insecurity, and fear, members of the queer community often flock to big cities where we can find ourselves and our chosen family. If we are lucky, confident, able, and willing, we may return to our small towns and communities, but more often than not, we call these new cities home. We flock to cities like DC, New York, San Francisco, Paris, Mexico City, and Cape Town, each with their own unique historically LGBTQ+ neighborhoods or districts or "Gay Villages." This may be why we have a hard time finding evidence of large gay rights movements in many countries around the world. Those who don't have a safe and prosperous "Gay Village" may resort to underground or undercover networks and codes to safely interact with one another. This was the case in the United States fifty years ago when there was no safe space for our community.

Homosexuality was not decriminalized in the United States until 2003 ("Lawrence v. Texas", 2003). That's over two-hundred years after the Declaration of Independence. You know who did decriminalize it over two-hundred years ago? France (Reuters, 2013). If France was the first country in the world to decriminalize homosexuality, then why isn't queer history told from the perspective of the French? How did the community's stories and history only seem to come from the perspective of the community that calls the US home?

Simply, the US currently, and for over a hundred years, controls the narrative.

With the Treaty of Paris of 1898 ending the Spanish-American War, the United States' position on the global stage changed dramatically (Library of Congress). By defeating Spain, it gained Cuba and Puerto Rico in the Caribbean and the Philippines, and Guam in the Pacific. According to the former Assistant Secretary of State, George L. Rives, this moment fundamentally shifted our stance to the point where the US "shall now and henceforth be looked upon as having cast aside [its] traditional attitude of isolation." (Department of State 1981). This moment unintentionally began to transfer the power of the pen over to the United States at the start of the 20th century and was solidified as the Great Wars fragmented and dissolved established empires into many of the countries we know of today. This change in global politics shifted the center of power quickly, and arguably until this day, to the United States. It is not at all strange for the leading global power to also be the one to control the historical narrative.

THE ANCIENT GAY AGENDA

If the United States is currently responsible for spreading the gay agenda, then the Ancient Greeks played a key role in developing and setting its priorities. Ancient Greeks not only accepted, but openly embraced a system of "marriage" or relationships, between older and younger consenting men, with the idea that the union wasn't always necessarily about love, but that it was more about mentorship, status, and knowledge (Davidson, 2007). Many of these relationships, most famously those of Achilles and Patroclus and Alexander the Great and Hephaestion, were so intense and depicted through epic poems and art in such a way that they lead to the conclusion of the existence of sexual relationships among men (Davidson, 2007). We know so much about the development of the Ancient Greek "gay agenda" because it was well documented. It wasn't something the Greeks ignored or tried to hide, and luckily for the rest of us, it is history that has survived. The leadership and impact of Alexander the Great is not something that could just be erased from history, even if he could have very likely been queer.

Homosexuality was so commonplace that even the great philosopher Plato spoke fondly about the relationship between two men. In one of his better-known and often discussed works, *Symposium,* Plato details how same-sex relationships came to be. After discussing what we know as heterosexual relationships and lesbians, he proceeds to discuss, at length and in great detail, relationships among men. He does so in such a way that defends these men's manliness. Not only did the ancient Greeks help develop the gay agenda, but clearly, they were the founders of toxic masculinity.

"But they who are a section of the male follow the male, and while they are young, being slices of the original man, they hang about men and embrace them, and they are themselves the best of boys and youths, because they have the most manly nature. Some indeed assert that they are shameless, but this is not true; for they do not act thus from any want of shame, but because they are valiant and manly, and have a manly countenance, and they embrace that which is like them."

Not only did Plato interpret homosexuality as "manly", "valiant", and nothing to be ashamed of, he spoke to the community's leadership ability and willingness to put country and obligations before the needs of oneself.

"And these when they grow up become our statesmen, and these only, which is a great proof of the truth of what I am saving. When they reach manhood they are loves of youth, and are not naturally inclined to marry or beget children,-if at all, they do so only in obedience to the law; but they are satisfied if they may be allowed to live with one another unwedded; and such a nature is prone to love and ready to return love, always embracing that which is akin to him."

Many of the assertions made by Plato may still ring true even in modern times. Given how hard it is, or how inconvenient, to have children, many couples focus on their careers and giving back to the community rather than having babies. Five years after marriage equality was passed in the United

States, it is estimated that 15 percent of Same-Sex couples have children compared to 38 percent of heterosexual couples (Schneider, 2020). Instead, there is a tendency to care for the wider community and look beyond the traditional interpretation of the family. Maybe it is because growing up we tend to be incredibly focused on our education, extracurriculars, and future. There is a drive to push the envelope. Even with discrimination and lack of protection in employment, LGBTQ+ couples are often more educated and have higher incomes than their heterosexual counterparts (Kurtzleben, 2013).

While same-sex relationships between men were not just tolerated, but a part of ancient Greek culture, relationships between two women aren't discussed to the same extent. While we may have the stories of Achilles and Alexander or the writings of Plato, among many others, to dive deeper into male homosexuality, we only have the lyricist and poet Sappho to look at relationships among women from a female perspective. Even within the broader community, not many know that Sappho, who was from the island of Lesbos, became synonymous with Lesbians and women who love women. Not much is known about Sappho, especially not to the same extent that is known about Achilles, Alexander the Great, or Plato. What we have learned, and therefore interpreted, comes from fragmented and incomplete poems found throughout history and records that depict her as both the "10th muse" but also as an "oversexed predator of men" (Mendelshon & Mead, 2015). There is a misogynistic undercurrent compounded by a lack of information.

Despite that deep, and even sexual, relationships among men were commonplace, the misogynistic undercurrent persisted.

There was still a tremendous amount of stigma between the different "roles" played by each man with a negative connotation, and later public implications for the one who played the "passive" role. For all the philosophy and art produced in Ancient Greece, they were constantly engaging in battles and wars with neighboring city-states. This kind of "victor" and loser mentality carries over to the relationship of the active and passive roles (Davidson, 2007).

Within the gay community, we still see a great deal of shaming and assumptions surrounding the roles played by men. Heteronormative roles, expectations, and categorizations still creep their undesired presence into LGBTQ+ relationships. There is an unnatural infatuation with the sexual role played by queer individuals and what that means, or how its interpreted, by heteronormative standards. Questions such as asking "who is the man and who is the woman in the relationship" are too common; as if washing the dishes, cooking, or mowing the lawn are limited to gender. My husband and I both wash the dishes, we both cook (one of us is better than the other though—yes, it's him), and we don't have a lawn to mow.

Very much at the speed of the DeLorean, history quickly morphs and transforms something that wasn't just common, but part of the higher echelons of society, into something unspeakable and illegal. By the time Europeans began exploring the world outside of their immediate frame of reference, homosexuality was long forgotten as part of their culture. Yes, they still remembered the Greeks and the Romans as part of the founding history of European civilization, but they had discarded their culture, systems of government, and customs in favor of those that fell in line with the rising strength of Christianity and imperialism. In 2015, Germany was the only European country on the list of top ten Christian countries according to Pew. By 2060, they predict that there will be no European country and instead six will be African nations (Diamant, 2019). When such explorers began to travel the globe and invade already inhabited land, they encountered other civilizations where the European sense of gender norms and relationships were not present.

Despite China's current stance on LGBTQ+ rights, their history, especially that dating back to the Han Dynasty (206 BC-220 AD) shows evidence of same-sex relationships (Zhang, 2015). It is commonly accepted that the majority of the Emperors of the Han Dynasty had both relationships with men and multiple wives, making bisexuality much more common throughout history than we think (Prager, 2020). It is likely, looking at the Greeks and Chinese, that bisexuality and the fluidity of relationships were more common than strictly heterosexual or homosexual relationships.

Fluidity is also commonly found in Ancient Indian texts where many epic stories are centered around women, gender-fluid, and transgender individuals. In the *Valmiki Ramayana*, an epic of ancient India, there are multiple stories of women in same-sex relationships and wives producing an heir after the death of King Dilip with the blessing of Lord Shiva (India Today, 2018). Transgender and gender-fluid individuals are depicted as fierce and brave warriors along with the multiple lords and gods whose gender is either fluid or frankly irrelevant (India Today, 2018). Current laws in India are the product of colonialism as are many of the laws and views against homosexuality worldwide (Kane, 2020). The fluidity of gender, gender roles, sexuality, and relationships depicted through the gods and stories of ancient India reinforce the narrative that it wasn't always a sin to be queer.

"DEVIANTS"

As history has taught us, because the Europeans held the power of the pen, these new cultures were seen as savage, pagan, and backward by the elite missionaries, diplomats, and anthropologists that shared stories from the Americas to the Orient. However, it seems that these early historians may have been more interested in producing a Stephen King novel rather than an accurate and unbiased representation of these cultures. Homosexuality isn't an on and off switch, and despite the great queer disappearance, we were very much there. Through attempts at "civilizing" the world to European standards, colonizers didn't just destroy civilizations by bringing disease wherever they went, but by actively erasing and deforming rich and accepting cultures in the name of Christianity.

It would be hard to make the argument that homosexuality was wrong if there was evidence of it everywhere. The more culture can attach its values to religion, especially when the ideology explicitly calls out homosexuality as sinful, the easier it is to make the moral argument against "sexual deviants." If this is then both the moral and literal law of the land, then it makes it easy, and legally justifiable, to rid yourself of the "gay problem." The penalty for homosexuality became death, so it's not hard to understand why we suddenly disappeared.

No, we weren't killed off, but the proverbial closet was invented. One would think that the Enlightenment period that questioned the role of the church in politics and sought reform would have given rise to a renaissance of LGBTQ+ inclusion. Instead, despite the increased visibility of homosexuality during this time through art and literature, beheading and burning at the stake were still part of the criminal code for homosexual acts (Stanley, 2004).

With the perceived role as the defender of human rights during and after the World Wars, the United States became the land of the free and the home of the brave. Immigrants began to flock to the United States with the same fundamental idea as the original settlers on the Mayflower—freedom from prosecution. It's unlikely that the United States set out to be the defender of the queers. We began to gain critical mass as a community and gathered enough allies to eventually begin to change the hearts and minds of society.

Regardless of all of the gaps throughout history, our presence has always been felt. Almost all civilizations, if not all, created and implemented laws that made something as critical to human survival as shelter, food, and water illegal—love. The LGBTQ+ community has been in existence since the foundation of our societies. Advancements in LGBTQ+ rights seem to be a phenomenon of the twenty-first century when, in reality, rights for all marginalized communities continues to be an ongoing battle even in the "advanced" western nations.

We are everywhere and nowhere throughout history, yet we are most visible through the laws set in place to literally remove us from existence. Through this, our presence is felt in the founding documents and laws of countries around the world and major religious texts. We have always been there, even if we have been met with restrictions in anticipation of the leaders that were to come from our community.

Our history is one of resilience, perseverance, and yes, a bit of good trouble. Otherwise, why would they have tried so hard to make us disappear?

3

Before There Was Pride There Was Prejudice

─────

Over the last one-hundred years, we have begun to see better record keeping of our community's presence. It was something that could no longer be ignored and something we began to fight for in increasingly public ways.

Pinpointing the birth of the modern-day "Gay Rights" movement is complicated. There isn't a moment in time that our community can point to and say, this was when it all started. Over the last one-hundred years is when we have had the most success for the Gay Agenda. A sort of "Gay Rights Greatest Hits." In 2021, we had the Equality Act once again reintroduced during the 117th Congress' legislative session. Before this, it was the fight for Marriage Equality and prior to that, it was the fight to repeal "Don't Ask Don't Tell." Further than that was the start of (and ongoing) AIDS pandemic. Most people would stop at the Stonewall Riots as the birth of the movement, but we can continue to go back in time throughout the 1900s and even into the late 1890s, when the rights of the LGBTQ+ community begun to take center stage.

Increased communication has helped pave the way for the fight for our rights. Interestingly, literacy rates and LGBTQ+ rights have had a similar upward trajectory during the same time period. Around the time that the first LGBTQ+ rights organization was founded in the United States in 1924, the literacy rate was 94 percent, however, it was only 77 percent for "Blacks and Others" (NCES). These were the same "Black and Others" who were fundamental in paving the way for so many LGBTQ+ rights movements in the US and whose culture has been adopted, without credit, by the larger community.

At the time of Harvey Milk's untimely death in 1979 (Milk Foundation), and the establishment of the Human Rights Campaign in 1980 (HRC), the literacy rate was 99.4 percent and 98.4 percent in the Black community (NCES). As literacy rates increased almost in tandem with the rising pressure by the media movement, information became easier to disseminate. This dramatically changed the nature of information sharing and record keeping. No longer reserved for only some members of society, news became available to the masses. This liberalization of communications has allowed the LGBTQ+ community to make its stories known and, most importantly, assure that these tales are told by us and for us.

BEFORE PRIDE

In 1924, the first gay rights organization was established in the United States in Chicago, Illinois by a German immigrant by the name of Henry Gerber ("Henry Gerber, 2019). Though short-lived, the Society for Human Rights was established with the idea to advocate for the rights of gays and lesbians. Gerber was inspired by the "homosexual emancipation movement" he saw while stationed in Germany as part of the US Military during World War I ("Henry Gerber", 2019). Though it was the first Lesbian and Gay rights organization in the United States, it met its end only a year after opening its doors to the public. In reality, those doors were firmly closed to a public that was not yet ready to accept such an organization.

One of the co-founders of the Society for Human Rights was outed by his wife for having "unnatural" tendencies and the entire organization was raided by police (Henry Gerber, 2019). Henry Gerber was fired from his 1920s respectable job at the post office and proceeded to spend his life savings in costly legal fees until eventually the case was dismissed. Despite these quite literal trials and tribulations, Henry still reenlisted as a member of the US Army for another seventeen years. He, like many other gay men at the time, carefully balanced his private life, considered unnatural and un-American by the public, with his very public persona as a member of the US Military—arguably one of the most patriotic things one can do for one's country.

Meanwhile, in Henry's home country of Germany, there was a movement trying to repeal a law known as "Paragraph 175," which made homosexual acts illegal. Paragraph 175 also criminalized bestiality, prostitution, and underage sexual abuse in the same law, as if all of these acts were subject to the same level of criminality (Broich, 2017). Bestiality and the abuse of minors are atrocities, but sex work is work and gay rights are human rights, therefore neither of these two are in the same category as the formers. Europe was experiencing the birth of the LGBTQ+ rights movement, and it was not a movement focused just on the more socially acceptable, or socially comprehensible, Lesbian and Gay members of the community.

Transgender individuals were front and center of the movement sweeping Germany. At this time, doctors and scientists were seeing homosexuality and "transvestism" as natural and not a medical anomaly that needed to be cured, but instead as one that needed to be understood (Broich, 2017). Controversial as it was for Eddie Redmayne to have played a trans character in the 2015 film *The Danish Girl,* it brought to the masses the story of Lili Elbe. Lili Elbe's story was one of the first well-documented gender confirmation surgeries in 1930 in Berlin, Germany (Keehnen, 2020). The initial surgery was performed by Dr. Magnus Hirschfeld, the founder of *Institut für Sexualwissenschaft,* or the Institute for Sexual Science, and a critical and early researcher and advocate for the understanding and research of LGBTQI persons (Djajic-Horváth, 2021). Lili's transition resulted in the annulment of her marriage to her wife Gerda by the King Christian X of Denmark, after she legally changed her name and was recognized as a woman (Djajic-Horváth, 2021).

Think about how wild it was that Lili could legally change her name and be recognized as a woman in the 1930s, yet in the twenty-first century, we are still struggling with letting trans kids play sports; mind-blowing. Sadly, Lili's life came to an end in 1931 when she died from complications of one of her surgeries to transplant uterine tissue. Her story of perseverance, resilience, and strength inspired many after her to find their truest identity and was one of the first times that the concept of gender was separated from sexual orientation.

However, there needs to be the right combination, not just of LGBTQ+ individuals in a place, but the ability to win the hearts and minds of the wider society. While the potential repeal of Paragraph 175 was making its round around the major cities of Europe at the time, like Paris and Vienna, there was still not enough community support. Instead of building support, the French press talked about the possibility of "the contagion corrupting society" (Sibalis, 2002), and in Germany, "obscene press material" (Marhoefer, 2015) being available to gay men which caused a response of fear and outrage. As a result of this hostile environment towards the LGBTQ+ community, many terrifying events soon unfolded throughout Germany and much of Europe.

THE PINK TRIANGLE

There are books, courses, and I'm sure, entire degrees that can be earned to understand the intricacies of the events that led to the rise of Hitler and the Nazis across Germany. The way we look at the events that created the environment for Hitler and his supporters to get away with all they did, will be the same way future generations will look at the forty-fifth president of the United States; with a sense of confusion and the question of, 'you really didn't see that coming?' Sure, we can blame much of what happened in Europe on the 1930s global depression, but can we really attribute the rise of nationalism in the United States and throughout Europe to the 2008 financial crisis? I'm sure time will tell, but if there is a grad student out there looking for an interesting thesis topic, here is one, free of charge.

Economic instability, combined with the rising trend of the 'us vs. them' mentality and fueled by increasingly polarizing political parties, required someone to blame. Yes, I promise I'm writing about the 1930s again and not referring to the year 2020. When the economic systems that have for so long held up systems of government begin to collapse, there always seems to be a scapegoat for the threat to traditional ways of life. As measures of austerity and a "toned-down" way of life began to take hold of much of the world during the Great Depression, the flamboyant and disruptive threat to morals and values that LGBTQ+ people apparently posed made them a prime target.

In May of 1933, three months after Hitler took power in Germany, the Institute for Sexual Science's collection of thousands of books and works was burned as part of the Nazi's campaign to rid itself of the "intellectual garbage of the past" (Schillace, 2021). All of this while Dr. Magnus Hirschfeld was away speaking in Switzerland. Some of the most famous images related to the ransacking and burning of books were from this Institute. History books don't often flag this. Kurt Hill, who was the Chair of the institute at the time, was eventually arrested for his role in promoting homosexuality and was sent to a concentration camp from where he, fortunately, later escaped (Fisher, 2009). Records from the Institute, such as the client list, were added to the "Pink List" and used to literally hunt gay men, resulting in the arrest of thousands in the next year alone (Sulzenbacher, 1999).

Unlike the Jewish community, members of the Communist party, and other targeted groups, there were no records or standards for what a "Gay" looked like or a membership roster (Giles, 2002). Lists, however, only give you a portion of the LGBTQ+ community. It very much takes one to know one. Aiding to the confusion of 'friend or foe,' and whether or not the queer community posed a threat to Hitler's plan, was the fact that many high-ranking members of the Nazi party were gay. Yes, LGBTQ+ individuals, specifically men, played a significant role in the persecution of millions during World War II. According to the United States Holocaust Memorial Museum, homophobia wasn't a problem among the Nazis, or even at the top of their list of groups to prosecute (Giles, 2002). As just mentioned, some of the top advisors and most loyal supporters of Hitler were openly gay. Germany itself was well on its way to abolishing Paragraph 175.

One of these men was Ernst Röhm, the head of the Sturm-abteilung (SA) Nazi paramilitary wing and Hitler's right-hand man. He was a strong opponent of Paragraph 175, and his sexuality appears to have been more common knowl-edge than many would expect (Wills, 2017). Another was a colleague of Dr. Magnus, Dr. Erwin Gohrbandt, who actu-ally helped perform the gender confirmation surgeries of Lili Elbe and Dora Richter (Schillace, 2021). Dr. Gohrbandt would later join the Luftwaffe, a wing of the Nazi military, and contribute to the human experiments conducted at the concentration camps.

Due to the influence and prevalence of gay men in the Nazi ranks, the "quick fix" implemented by the Nazis on other unwanted groups could not be as easily carried out without first acknowledging that the Nazi party, and its highest leadership, was gay. This would mean going after those who were 'racially pure' and benefited the race. If gay men were allowed to exist openly in society, then Hitler ran the risk of losing support from conservatives and weakening his argument. By the time the Sturmabteilung no longer served their purpose, neither did Röhm, and he was executed during the Night of Long Knives (Onion, Sullivan, Mullen, 2010). Hitler could now continue to use homosexuality as an excuse to murder thousands and send millions to concentration camps.

Resilience is just as much about leading as it is about surviving. There are moments and spaces, even to this day, where the resilience of the LGBTQ+ community is evident not just in the social movements or pride parades, but in simply having the will and skills to survive in a place that quite literally wants you dead. As Germany quickly descended into hell on earth for multiple minority groups deemed morally wrong, many LGBTQ+ individuals went back into the closet by marrying members of the opposite sex in an effort to blend in (Heger, 2010). Those who refused or were easily recognized by the Nazis as being leaders of the community, were sent to concentration camps and branded with a pink triangle (Heger, 2010).

During Nazi Germany, this pink triangle became a way to signal out gay men in the concentration camps. Not only did these men face incredible abuse and experimentation, but they were also ostracized from other prisoners of the camp for not being "normal." There is a story of a survivor who managed to swap his pink triangle for a red one, meaning he was a communist instead of a homosexual, in order to avoid the abuse and experiments that attempted to "cure" gay men (Heger, 2010). Though the pink triangle has been reclaimed and repurposed by the LGBTQ+ community as a symbol of pride, the community still faces unjust experimentation through unwanted and unneeded medical practices such as forced conversion therapy and unconsented surgeries on intersex individuals.

THE LAVENDER SCARE

After the atrocities of World War II, the world was still not ready to accept the LGBTQ+ community even though LGBTQ+ servicemen and women played a key role in the war effort. After the attacks on Pearl Harbor "whatever attitudes [were] had about non-involvement immediately disappeared and [LGBTQ people] became as much a part of the war effort as everyone else" (Foreman, 2020). Aside from being a patriotic thing to do, joining the military actually gave many LGBTQ+ individuals the opportunity to realize that they weren't alone.

You know how parents don't allow their kids to sleepover at the houses of those of the opposite sex but would let their kids spend the night at the house of a kid of the same sex? Well, imagine this on a mass scale, but as adults in the military. As men and women poured into the military, they found themselves around their own gender 24/7, allowing them to form bonds and relationships. The Women's Army Auxiliary Corp unknowingly featured Phyllis Abry and her partner in one of their campaigns to promote the ideal image of women in the military (Foreman, 2020).

Even though the United States had witnessed the devastation across Europe and knew about the human rights violations occurring in the concentration camps, this did not change how it treated its own citizens. The LGBTQ+ community was demonized and discriminated against despite their contributions towards ending the war. Many were given a blue discharge from the military, meaning they were unfit to serve, instead of an honorable discharge. This was also used disproportionately on Black service-members (Foreman, 2020). As part of America's efforts to purge itself of communists in the federal government during what is known as the *red scare*, it also used this moment to oust LGBTQ+ government employees in the lesser known *lavender scare* (Gleason, 2017).

Imagine being called into a meeting by your boss, their boss, and some lawyers in a dark, smokey room—pretty sure that is not the setting of an upcoming pay raise or promotion. Instead, LGBTQ+ individuals were interrogated about their personal lives, deviant tendencies, and "perversions." LGBTQ+ employees of the federal government posed a threat because if they could live double lives in public and private, then they could just as easily be spies for the Soviets. At least, this was the mentality. In 1953, President Eisenhower signed Executive Order 10450, banning "any criminal, infamous, dishonest, immoral, or notoriously disgraceful conduct, habitual use of intoxicants to excess, drug addiction, sexual perversion" from the federal government (Exec. Order. 10450). Though an exact number is unknown, it is estimated that between five and ten thousand queer federal employees were terminated (Haynes, 2020).

Working to make the federal government more inclusive and representative of LGBTQ+ individuals isn't simply a privilege, but it's an honor to rewrite the wrongs of decades of discrimination.

PRIDE AND PROTEST – 1969

Martin Duberman, author of *Stonewall*, shares that the culture of the 1950s and 1960s despised the LGBTQ+ community. It was common to hear phrases like, "you're second class," "you're disturbed," and "you're an arbitration" during this time (Waxman, Lautrup, 2019). This was also happening against the backdrop of the Civil Rights movement of the 1960s —a time defined by rebellion, the feminist movement, and slogans such as "black is beautiful," which Duberman says sparked an awakening within the community (Waxman, Lautrup, 2019).

During this time, raids on businesses that catered to the LGBTQ+ community were commonplace. Often during these raids was the enforcement of the 'three-piece law,' which could get anyone arrested who was not wearing three pieces of clothing that matched their gender assigned at birth. Though this law was not one that was technically in the books, it was often used throughout the era of the Civil Rights movement to target the Queer community. Multiple police reports make mentions to the fact that individuals at these establishments were in violation of a non-existent law "and since socks didn't count" according to Martin Boyce, a patron of the Stonewall, they often checked articles of clothing past shirts and jeans (Lucero, 2019). Even in the United States, the LGBTQ+ community felt prosecuted and hunted down by the same police force that was there to protect them in the first place.

Our country has had a long and ongoing, history of police brutality towards marginalized communities.

It was because of, not despite, the intersection of race and sexuality that the Stonewall riots came to be. On June 28, 1969, riots broke out at the Stonewall Inn in New York. Like many times before, police had raided the bar, but unlike other times, the community had had enough. Constant discrimination, harassment, and prosecution by the police had reached a tipping point. Plus, it likely didn't help that it happened to be a particularly hot summer night and by many accounts this likely, and quite literally, added fuel to the fire that was to come (Pruitt, 2019).

Marsha P. Johnson, a black woman, was a self-identified Drag Queen dubbed the Mayor of Christopher Street, the street on which the Stonewall Inn is located. Despite going by Marsha, the P in her name stood for "pay it no mind." (MPJI) which was in reference to her response to questions about her gender. By many accounts of people present that night, it was Johnson, a well-known member of the LGBTQ+ community in the Village, who may have possibly thrown the first brick, or shot glass, towards the bar. According to the story, this caused the glass of the mirror behind it to shatter, essentially sparking a series of events that would set the Gay rights movement in motion with the same intensity as the cracks on that now shattered mirror (Pruitt, 2019).

In many ways, the Stonewall Riots are part of the great mythology of the gay rights movement—a sort of oral tradition passed down by those who were actually there. Some say that what ignited the mob and turned them into a riot was Stormé DeLarverie. DeLarverie was known for her androgynous performances at first and then later as the "guardian of lesbians in the Village" (Yardley, 2014). Police attempted to take DeLarverie into custody after arresting her for dressing and performing in men's clothing, but during this attempt, she complained about the pain the handcuffs were causing, which then ignited the crowd to come to her defense. This resulted in items being thrown at the police (Pruitt, 2019). It's unsure if DeLarverie was in fact the woman being arrested that night or, if as others say, she threw the first punch against the police as they attempted to put her in custody (Yardley, 2014).

Another significant presence at the start of the riots, even if was more or less in myth and mystique, was Sylvia Rivera. A Venezuelan-Puerto Rican American, Rivera was another prominent figure in the village and a close friend of Johnson's (Rothberg, 2021). Similar in many ways, both fought for the rights of all LGBTQ+ individuals without necessarily choosing to identify with one group or another. Both mainly referred to themselves as drag queens, or performers, despite now being labeled as founders of not just the LGBTQ+ rights movement as a whole, but the trans movement before the term transgender was commonly used (Rothberg, 2021).

Three people of color paved the way, or threw the first brick that paved the way, for the entire rainbow of identities to have a seat at the table.

Stonewall sparked the first riot or rebellion for the rights of LGBTQ+ individuals who were just trying to live their lives. The Stonewall Inn became the gathering spot not just for LGBTQ+ individuals, but also activists as early as the following day. Supporters gathered chanting "gay power" and "we shall overcome" and the police were immediately called to put out the protest (Pruitt, 2019). A year later as a commemoration of the riot, activists gathered and organized the "Christopher Street Liberation March" in which people marched toward Central Park, giving birth to the Pride Parade (Pruitt, 2019). The first pride was nothing like what we are used to seeing now, but the first pride also wasn't a riot. It was a reflection of the fight ahead for a community desperate to be allowed to exist.

The Stonewall riots have as much fact as they do fiction around them, maybe to the same extent that Marsha and Sylvia do. Together they are part of the epic poem that we call the Gay Rights Movement. The movement may have already been growing, with individuals at multiple stages laying their own brick on the path towards civil rights we have achieved so far, but Stonewall continues, and will continue to be the spark that ignited a generation. Our collective history is difficult and often sad, but Stonewall is the moment in time that our history took a sharp turn. It is at this point in time that we were no longer solely the victims of an oppressive system, and we began to learn to harness our resilience to do more than simply live and survive. We learned how to thrive and make it known that we're here and we're queer; get used to it!

4

The AIDS Pandemic

Now I'm going to age myself here, and not in the direction that you think. My generation is unaware of and takes for granted the tremendous advancements gained by the LGBTQ+ community as a result of the activism of the 1980s. A small portion of my generation caught the tail end of the fight for marriage equality—yes we celebrated it —but we weren't at the forefront of that fight. Our fight continues building on the legwork by the generations before us, but we take too much for granted.

The AIDS pandemic that began in the early 1980s had become a part of life for the LGBTQ+ community and shaped popular perception about our community. It was a disease that many, to this day, believe targets and seeks out those who "deserve it" in society. When I came out in 2015, thirty-five years after the start of the pandemic, my parents were concerned for my safety. Living in DC didn't mean that my parents were afraid that my coming out would result in a potential hate crime, but that they worried I'd get HIV/AIDS because they grew up in the 1980s.

America clearly didn't learn much from the AIDS pandemic. We should have studied it as part of our formal education. No, not because it's LGBTQ+ history, that would be too progressive of a curriculum, but because it is crucial to understanding how not to handle a pandemic. We saw stigmatization of minority communities, delayed government action, and avoidance of advocating for and reinforcing accessible preventative methods. These are all things we should have known to avoid and to combat at the start of the COVID-19 pandemic.

If only we had looked at the AIDS pandemic that started in the 1980s and is still raging globally today, maybe COVID-19 wouldn't have gotten out of hand. Maybe we wouldn't have had a President and administration stigmatizing the Asian community by calling the virus the "China virus." If only Trump would have taken swift action to stop the spread and we had all worn our masks when told to do so. I'm sorry, but Dr. Fauci was there during the AIDS pandemic, and he was in the White House since the start of the COVID-19 pandemic. Did he not draw these parallels, or was he simply ignored by yet another Republican president?

LOSING A GENERATION

In June of 1981, the Center for Disease Control (CDC) published the first article on a novel lung infection, Pneumocystis Carinii Pneumonia (PCP) in the Morbidity and Mortality Weekly Report (MMWR) ("A Timeline of HIV and AIDS," 2021). What was particularly interesting about the disease was not the fact that you could essentially talk about it as just acronyms, but the fact that it had infected "five young, white, previously healthy gay men." ("A Timeline of HIV and AIDS," 2021). Simultaneously, reports were coming out of New York about a particularly fast-acting cancer, Kaposi's Sarcoma (KS), which had also seemed to be found uniquely in gay men (Tanne, 2008). Stories of these cases traveled quickly within the LGBTQ+ community, of what was seeming like an opportunistic virus targeting an already marginalized community group. By July, twenty-six more cases were confirmed and "gay cancer" was wrongfully embedded into the minds of mainstream society ("A Timeline of HIV and AIDS," 2021).

As the summer of 1981 came to an end, seventy additional cases had been confirmed, bringing the total to one-hundred and eight. Of these, one-hundred and seven were male, 94 percent of them were gay or bisexual men, and 40 percent of those infected died ("A Timeline of HIV and AIDS," 2021). By the end of the year, there were three-hundred and seventy-seven reported cases, including sixteen for children under the age of thirteen. There were already signs that the new virus was showing up in newborns, making it difficult to label the new disease simply as the gay virus, but doctors at the time dismissed and misdiagnosed these children (Tanne, 2008).

By May 1982, the New York Times published an article titled New Homosexual Disorder Worries Health Officials and began to utilize the term "Gay-Related Immune Deficiency" (GRID) making it the dominant reference to what would eventually be a global pandemic (Altman, 1982). It wasn't until September of the same year that the term Acquired Immune Deficiency Syndrome (AIDS) would be first mentioned by the CDC ("A Timeline of HIV and AIDS," 2021).

For over two years, the blame of the virus was placed squarely on the LGBTQ+ community and specifically homosexual men. History had already made it difficult for members of the community to advance in their personal lives and careers without being blamed for a literal pandemic.

Wait, blaming a group for a pandemic when they have nothing to do with it? Sounds familiar. Already marginalized, the LGBTQ+ community was further ostracized and cast aside for no other reason than pure ignorance, which cost thousands of lives. It wasn't until 1983, two years after the start of the pandemic, that the *New York Times* would finally mention AIDS on the front page (Pear, 1983).

So what did the LGBTQ+ community do when no one wanted to help? When so many died alone and isolated because misinformation made people believe that AIDS could be transmitted through a hug? Who did we turn to? Ourselves.

In a time of great terror, that seemed as if by intentional divine intervention according to some, our community became just that, a community. Larry Kramer was one of the first individuals who used his network as a famous writer and film producer to hold a meeting in New York City within weeks of the news of the novel virus (Kennedy, 2020).

At this first meeting, he helped raise some of the only new research money invested at the time to understand this novel "cancer" that was impacting the gay community. This meeting would eventually lead to the foundation of the Gay Men's Health Crisis (GMHC), founded by Kramer along with

Nathan Fain, Lawrence Mass, Paul Popham, Paul Rapport, and Edmund White (History, 2020). It was the community that raised the money and the community that first cared about finding a cure, when the rest of the world was using it to alienate queers for being "immoral" and "deadly." This community exists to this day – we have our support, our chosen family.

The White House, under President Ronald Reagan, refused to take the raging virus as anything but a joke. During a White House Press Briefing in 1982, Lester Kinsolving was the first reporter to ask US Press Secretary Larry Speakes about AIDS and the conversation went like this:

Lester Kinsolving: *Does the president have any reaction to the announcement by the Centers for Disease Control in Atlanta that AIDS is now an epidemic in over 600 cases?*

US Press Secretary Speakes: *AIDS? I haven't got anything on it.*

Lester: *Over a third of them have died. It's known as the "gay plague."* [Press pool laughter.] *No, it is. It's a pretty serious thing. One in every three people that get this have died. And I wonder if the president was aware of this.*

US Press Secretary Speakes: *I don't have it.* [Press pool laughter.] *Do you?*

Lester: *You don't have it? Well, I'm relieved to hear that, Larry!* [Press pool laughter.]

US Press Secretary Speakes: *Do you?*

Lester: *No, I don't.*

US Press Secretary: *You didn't answer my question. How do you know?* [Press pool laughter.]

Lester: *Does the president — in other words, the White House — look on this as a great joke?*

US Press Secretary: *No, I don't know anything about it, Lester* (Lopez, 2015).

Various other questions about the developing pandemic were met with homophobia and ridicule by Lester Kinsolving. US Press Secretary Speakes and the press pool often used the Kinsolving's questions about the AIDS crisis to make fun of or discredit the LGBTQ+ community, dismissing a health crisis that couldn't have been cured, but could have been mitigated. They seemed to be more concerned about Kinsolving's personal connection to the "fairies" as referred to in one press briefing rather than answering the real question (Lopez, 2015).

The White House, that beacon of democracy and America, the symbol of "freedom and justice for all," was the least concerned with the developing pandemic given that they had "never heard of it" or "didn't know anything about it." Due to a lack of direction, empathy, or concern for thousands of Americans, a disease they had never heard of would account for over 100,000 deaths during Ronald Regan's term as president of the United States from 1981 to 1989 ("A Timeline of HIV and AIDS," 2021).

Larry Kramer, the same man who founded GMHC, eventually resigned from the board in 1983, disappointed that GMHC was not doing enough, was not loud enough, and was not angry enough to truly get the attention of the decision-makers and holders of the purse strings (Kennedy, 2020). So, he left and founded the AIDS Coalition to Unleash Power (ACT UP) in 1987 (Kennedy, 2020). This organization was and continues to be vocal, proactive, and political. ACT UP's motto became "Silence = Death" or in other words, if you aren't with us, you're against us. The organization was part knowledge gathering and understanding the ongoing pandemic and part civil disobedience in how they protested. David France, author of *How to Survive a Plague*, described the organization's success as being "not just the anger. But the anger coupled with intelligence" (Aizenman, 2019).

ACT UP would be strategic in their unapologetic confrontation. They would target organizations, government agencies, and individuals who held the pen in the legislative process or who held the ear of society. Most memorable of these protests were the "die-ins" in front of the Food and Drug Administration (FDA), Wall Street, and St. Patrick Cathedral. Essentially the state, the money, and the church, together, were responsible for the tremendous misinformation directed at the queer community and lack of research funding. These institutions were blamed for the deaths of thousands including many of the members of ACT UP. They weren't shy about it either, quite literally saying "stop killing us" or "killed by the FDA," but most famously "If I died of AIDS —forget the burial —just drop my body on the steps of the F.D.A" (Aizenman, 2019). Once they had been able to get the attention of the decision-makers through newsworthy activism, those organizations, such as the FDA, had no choice but to take a meeting with the organization.

THE QUILT

Much of the activism and organizations started by the LGBTQ+ community in the face of the AIDS pandemic still exist today including ACT UP, which is still active. With so much loss came the need to create a space to remember and heal. This became the NAMES Project AIDS Memorial Quilt or the AIDS Quilt. Cleve Jones, an LGBTQ+ rights activist who helped organize the annual candlelit march in San Francisco commemorating the death of Harvey Milk and Mayor Moscone, came up with the idea for a patchwork representation of the lives lost to the AIDS pandemic. During the Milk-Moscone commemorative march, he learned about the thousands of lives already lost to the pandemic. At this march, people took paper placards and signs, wrote the names of friends, loved ones, chosen family members on them, and covered the front of the San Francisco Federal Building. This patchwork of names on the building inspired Jones and, in 1987, the quilt began to take shape ("The History of the Quilt").

The AIDS Quilt consists of a series of panels that are three feet by six feet, or roughly the size of a grave, to illustrate the sheer space that the number of US AIDS-related deaths would take up. These panels are then sewn together in a block of eight and this is how they are displayed. In October of 1987, the Second National March on Washington for Lesbian and Gay Rights presented the perfect venue to show to the Clinton administration the magnitude of the pandemic ("The History of the Quilt").

In 1987, the AIDS Quilt included 1,920 panels and took up more space than a football field on the National Mall. Just a year later, the quilt was back in Washington, this time with more than six thousand new panels for a total of 8,288. This time the quilt took up the entirety of The Ellipse, a fifty-two-acre park in front of the White House. By 1992, the quilt returned to DC, this time with twenty thousand panels moving from The Ellipse over to the surrounding area by the Washington Monument. By 1994, the number of AIDS cases in the US had surpassed 400,000 and had become the leading cause of death of Americans ages twenty-five to forty-four (*The Plague of Our Time*, 2012).

When the quilt returned to Washington DC just four years later in 1996, the quilt was composed of forty-thousand panels, taking up the entirety of the National Mall in Washington, DC, between the US Capitol and the Washington Monument. President Clinton and then First Lady Hillary Clinton, along with Vice President Gore and the Second Lady, visited the quilt, making it the first time a sitting US President visited the memorial.

In 2012, the AIDS Quilt celebrated its twenty-fifth anniversary as part of the NAMES Project, the Atlanta-based organization taking care of the maintenance and display of the quilt. At this point, the quilt was too large to be displayed solely on the National Mall. With over forty-eight thousand panels, it was over fifty miles long if laid end to end. Shockingly, the AIDS Quilt only represents 20 percent of the AIDS deaths in the United States alone. Globally, it is estimated that there are thirty-eight million people living with HIV/AIDS and deaths have been reduced by 60 percent since their peak in 2004. Though there has been as much as a one-fourth drop in HIV cases since 2010, there are still over half a million deaths each year due to complications related to HIV/AIDS ("A Timeline of HIV and AIDS," 2021).

Even only representing 20 percent of US-specific AIDS deaths, the quilt weighs fifty-four tons and is the largest piece of community folk art in the world. But more than breaking records, the AIDS Quilt is a reminder of the sense of community present among those who identify as LGBTQ+. It is a constant reminder that in times of darkness, in times of fear, and in times of hopelessness, we have a chosen family towards which to turn. A family we have built not through blood, but struggle and an understanding of the common adversity faced by each one of us blessed to be part of this vibrant and diverse community.

As the AIDS pandemic raged on, the LGBTQ+ community began to find its collective strength. The Stonewall riots gave us pride in both the literal and figurative sense and thanks to Stonewall, we now have a date, even a whole month, dedicated to recognizing the achievements of the community. Just the same, it is also a reason to take to the streets each year, demanding that we are seen, heard, and taken seriously.

The AIDS pandemic came off the heels of the National March on Washington for Lesbian and Gay Rights of 1979, one of the first times our community had come together to advocate for change at the highest levels. For that march to be followed and contradicted by the lack of response by the federal government illustrated just how resilient the LGBTQ+ community needed to be and how important it was for us to have a constant seat at the decision-making table. Centuries of laws were in place to stop us from being the political, cultural, business, and societal force for good that we could be. It was time to change that.

5

Legalizing Resilience

_____

If HIV/AIDS didn't stop you from living your life in the 1980s, then the laws that were enacted after would make it difficult to truly live your life out and proud.

DON'T ASK, DON'T TELL

As the AIDS pandemic became a part of the metaphorical and literal fabric of the LGBTQ+ community, we found ways to cope with the loss. Thanks to, in no small part, the pressure of the queer community, medical advancements meant that contracting HIV/AIDS was no longer a death sentence. The 1980s changed our community for the better; it made us resilient, it empowered us to be activists and leaders. Boy, would we need that over the next thirty years.

The country had noticed that we were queer and very much here, but it didn't seem that they were willing to get used to it. There have always been laws in place to prohibit the advancement of the LGBTQ+ community and, in the 1990s, new laws came into place in the United States that further attempted to reinforce the narrative of "you're a threat to societal standards." Signed into law in 1993 by President Clinton, "Don't Ask, Don't Tell" became the law of the land and the law for LGBTQ+ individuals serving in the United States Armed Forces (Pruitt, 2018). By becoming law, it reversed the forty-year-old Executive Order 10450 by President Eisenhower, which had previously made it illegal for those with "sexual perversions" from working in the government or joining the armed forces ("Exec. Order No. 10450 Fed. Reg. 2489"). Now, this didn't mean that you could serve as an openly queer individual, but that if you were willing to go back into the closet and not tell anyone, then the military wouldn't ask and would look the other way.

You would think that coming off from the Gulf War and our continued involvement in conflicts in the Middle East and elsewhere would mean that the United States would be proud to take any and all those willing to make the ultimate sacrifice for this country. Well, the queers were now welcome as long as they kept their sexuality to themselves and didn't give off any indication that they weren't straight. Though President Bill Clinton may have publicly shown his acknowledgment of the AIDS crisis, that didn't mean he had every best intention for the LGBTQ+ community.

So, the AIDS pandemic was raging, putting members of the community in hospitals and eventually into coffins while at the same time, the administration was willing to put us on the front lines as long as we stayed in the closet. Service members lived a double life, unable to disclose or refer to being LGBTQ+, and engaging in "homosexual activity" was out of the question (Pruitt, 2018). Intended to incentivize people to join the military, this "liberal" policy actually resulted in the discharge of more than thirteen-thousand service members by the end of 2009 as the US escalated its operations across the Middle East (Pruitt, 2018).

When the attempted repeal of "Don't Ask Don't Tell" was blocked by Senate Republicans in 2010, President Clinton had this to say in an interview with Katie Couric, "When Colin Powell sold me on 'don't ask, don't tell,' here's what he said it would be: Gay service members would never get in trouble for going to gay bars, marching in gay rights parades as long as they weren't in uniform. That's a very different don't ask, don't tell than we got."

Central to President Obama's 2008 campaign was the promise that he would repeal this law. It took him almost an entire term to fulfill this promise, but Congress finally passed the "Don't Ask Don't Tell Repeal Act of 2010" in December of that year (Lee, 2010).

If we have learned anything, it is that as soon as you have something, it can be taken away. As part of the efforts to repeal "Don't Ask Don't Tell," a study was conducted by the Pentagon of the potential disruption of changing this policy on the troops. It concluded that there would be "positive, mixed, or no consequence at all" of allowing LGBTQ+ individuals to openly serve in the military (Bumiller, 2010). The study went on to say that those instances of "disruption" would be addressed by effective leadership rather than the discharge of an asset. Despite the study, polling, and public announcement by the Department of Defense, all expressing no concern over any impact on the power and strength of the US Armed Forces, our community came under attack by the forty-fifth commander in chief.

In 2017, the record-holding, twice impeached, then-President of the United States, Donald Trump, once again mistook Twitter's 280 characters for an Executive Order. I sincerely hope that someone at some point told him this was a bad idea, but even so, on July 26, 2017 he tweeted:

"After consultation with my Generals and military experts, please be advised that the United States Government will not accept or allow transgender individuals to serve in any capacity in the US Military. Our military must be focused on decisive and overwhelming victory and cannot be burdened with the tremendous medical costs and disruption that transgender in the military would entail. Thank you." (Thompson, 2019).

Words have power, and these strung together in a tweet sparked confusion and rebellion within the ranks of the Department of Defense. For the rest of Trump's administration, transgender individuals would not be allowed to enlist. The Transgender Military Ban was repealed by Executive Order by President Biden within his first week in office thus "enabling all qualified Americans to serve their country in uniform." (Biden, 2021).

Serving in the Army, Navy, Marines, Air Force, Coast Guard, even the Space Force— yes it exists— is a choice and a sacrifice anyone may be willing to make. Its membership should not be limited by the lack of information, fear, and demonization of the LGBTQ+ community.

DEFENSE OF MARRIAGE ACT AND MARRIAGE EQUALITY

It seems that President Clinton was on a role. He had signed *Don't Ask Don't Tell* into law in a failed attempt to encourage LGBTQ+ service members to serve their country. Now having said that, President Clinton's Georgetown education must have flown out the door when he signed the Defense of Marriage Act (DOMA) in 1996. He must have known, or at least speculated, that something that defined marriage in such a binary way would be controversial and the Defense of Marriage Act did exactly what it sounds like it did, defend marriage; but only for a few.

"No State, territory, or possession of the United States, or Indian tribe, shall be required to give effect to any public act, record, or judicial proceeding of any other State, territory, possession, or tribe respecting a relationship between persons of the same sex that is treated as a marriage under the laws of such other State, territory, possession, or tribe, or a right or claim arising from such relationship" (H.R. 3396, Sec. 2, 1996).

It went on to further define marriage and spouse.

"In determining the meaning of any Act of Congress, or of any ruling, regulation, or interpretation of the various administrative bureaus and agencies of the United States, the word 'marriage' means only a legal union between one man and one woman as husband and wife, and the word 'spouse' refers only to a person of the opposite sex who is a husband or a wife." (H.R. 3396, Sec. 3, 1996).

Curious, since after signing DOMA in September of 1996, the president and first lady visited the AIDS Quilt while on display at the National Mall just a month later. Did they look at each other and think that marriage had an impact on the AIDS crisis?

Both the former president and former secretary of state now fully, and publicly, support marriage equality and LGBTQ+ rights. Hillary Clinton has, by many standards of the queer community, achieved the status of "Gay Icon" (Chozick, 2015). Maybe this is just by the pantsuits standards. During an interview with Rachel Maddow on MSNBC then Presidential candidate Hillary Clinton shared her view as to why DOMA was signed into law.

"There was enough political momentum to amend the Constitution of the United States of America [to define marriage] and there had to be some way to stop that. And there wasn't any rational argument because I was in on some of those discussions, about DADT and DOMA, where both the President and his advisors, and occasionally I, would chime in and say, 'you can't be serious, you can't be serious,' but they were. So, in a lot of ways DOMA was the line that was drawn to prevent going forward [and amending the Constitution]. It was a defensive action. The culture rapidly changed so that now what was totally anathema to political forces, they have ceded they no longer are fighting except on a local level. With the US Supreme Court decision, it is settled."

In fact, DOMA did pass both the House of Representatives and the US Senate with an overwhelming majority (Ramsey, 2013). So much so that even with a veto by President Clinton, it would have likely had enough support by Congress to be overturned and the law passed regardless. #Democracy.

Before full marriage would be passed, twelve states across the nation had already reformed their laws, paving the pathway towards national recognition (Honan, 2013). Parts of DOMA would be struck down, but full equality would have to wait. Marriage equality would not be achieved until the Supreme Court ruled on *Obergefell v. Hodges*. It took winning the hearts, minds, and eventually the case before the Supreme Court, to grant our community the simple right to marry who we loved. In the landmark five to four decision, marriage became legal for all Americans, not just some. Justice Anthony Kennedy delivered the Opinion of the Court in which he was joined by Justices Sotomayor, Ginsburg, Kagan, and Breyer.

"No union is more profound than marriage, for it embodies the highest ideals of love, fidelity, devotion, sacrifice, and family. In forming a marital union, two people become something greater than once they were. As some of the petitioners in these cases demonstrate, marriage embodies a love that may endure even past death. It would misunderstand these men and women to say they disrespect the idea of marriage. Their plea is that they do respect it, respect it so deeply that they seek to find its fulfillment for themselves. Their hope is not to be condemned to live in loneliness, excluded from one of civilization's oldest institutions. They ask for equal dignity in the eyes of the law. The Constitution grants them that right. The judgment of the Court of Appeals for the Sixth Circuit is reversed. It is so ordered." (Obergefell v. Hodges).

On June 26, 2015, the Supreme Court made its ruling on the case, right at the end of Pride month, as if to be the final sendoff. Down on Pennsylvania Avenue, the White House was lit up in the colors of the Pride flag, that iconic image. The feeling that overcame Washington as crowds gathered around the White House was a true "victory for America" that "made our union a little more perfect" as President Obama put it (Neuman, 2015).

I share all this knowing very well that I wasn't in DC at the time but instead walking through the Luxembourg Gardens in Paris on my study abroad, struggling to come to terms with my own sexuality. Timing, both biologically and in my own journey, made DOMA, DADT, and even marriage equality, the struggle and fight of another generation. Yet, I have benefited from the outcomes of progress. My career is centered around leadership development and primarily around the concept of ensuring representation for the LGBTQ+ and other marginalized communities in appointed and elected offices. Without the tremendous work of the activists, service members, and those on the ground fighting the good fight to repeal DADT, I wouldn't have a career. I would not be advocating for the first transgender ambassador or the first LGBTQ+ justice on the Supreme Court because it wouldn't be possible. Being part of the successful efforts to open a pathway to have the first LGBTQ+ Senate confirmed cabinet member and the first transgender appointee to a US government agency would seem like far off dreams without the advocacy of the leaders before me.

By the time I met my husband, Juan, marriage equality was commonplace. We didn't think, especially in a city like DC, that we would be discriminated against when looking at venues, caterers, and various vendors for our wedding. We had the wedding of our dreams, which perfectly combined our cultural identities as Latinos— he is Venezuelan— and our identity as members of the LGBTQ+ community. We were married on June 1, 2019, the first day of Pride month, at the Congressional Club in Washington, DC.

The Congressional Club has historically been a venue for "non-partisan setting for friendship among the spouses of members of the House and Senate" and has been the host for the First Lady's Luncheon, and hopefully one day the First Gentleman's too (The Congressional Club Museum and Foundation, 2020). The irony that two gay Latino immigrants were married at the Congressional Club during the Trump administration is not lost on Juan and me. Neither is the fact that we almost lost the venue to Melania's luncheon that year. Keyword: almost.

WHAT'S NEXT? THE EQUALITY ACT – 202?

We protect our children from abusive labor laws through the Fair Labor Standards Act. We protect those with disabilities through the Americans with Disabilities Act. We outlaw discrimination based on race, color, religion, sex, or national origin since the introduction of the Civil Rights Act of 1964. Yet, lesbian, gay, bisexual, transgender, and queer Americans go every day without the same protections as others in this country, simply because of who they are and who they love. How can the United States be founded on a principle of equality if we continue to legally allow for the discrimination of LGBTQ+ Americans?

It is time to give everyone in America a fighting chance and an even playing field. It is time to pass the Equality Act.

The Equality Act has been introduced in each and every session of Congress since 2015. If ever passed, it would amend critical pieces of legislation and increase the right and protections of all LGBTQ+ Americans. Currently, not all states protect against LGBTQ+ discrimination in federally funded programs or public spaces and services. It is still legal in twenty-two states for LGBTQ+ individuals to be denied service at a hotel, restaurant, flower shop, or bakery based on religious beliefs (MAP, 2021). Texas and Virginia are both states where entities can seek exemptions if it "burdens" their religion. In Alabama, this is part of their state constitution, but they aren't as bad as Mississippi, which can not only allow local officials to deny a marriage license, but also deny service to married same-sex couples (MAP, 2021). Too many opportunities for discrimination are left up to the interpretation of each state because they have not been defined or protected at the federal level.

Key pieces of historical US legislation such as the Civil Rights Act of 1964 and the Fair Housing Act would be updated to prohibit discrimination on the basis of sexual orientation and gender identity. This expands the rights for all. Anti-discrimination protections in employment, housing, credit, education, public spaces and services, federally funded programs, and jury service would also be included with the passing of the Equality Act (Kurtzleben, 2021). Explicitly including protections on the basis of sexual orientation and gender identity in fundamental laws in our country can guarantee that LGBTQ+ people have the same protections as other designated groups under federal law.

Some will argue that the LGBTQ+ community has made historic advancements in recent years, especially with the passing of same-sex marriage, but in most states this community still lacks basic legal protections against discrimination. Every day, millions of LGBTQ+ Americans face the risk of being denied a home or a job just because of their sexual orientation or gender identity. In most states, a same-sex couple can get married one day and fired the next just because of who they love. We need a federal law that protects all LGBTQ+ Americans.

The LGBTQ+ community is not the only one who would benefit from the passing of this bill, as expanding protections is not a trade-off between one group and the next. With increased protections, other marginalized communities also win by demanding an end to the systematic discrimination of all minority communities. The Equality Act seeks to add specific mentions of protections based on sex and gender identity. By adding this, women would also be protected in areas that don't explicitly mention it. When LGBTQ+ rights are protected, women's rights are protected, and communities of color are protected. LGBTQ+ rights are human rights and human rights are LGBTQ+ rights. The Equality Act would make it clear that religion is not a license to discriminate.

Protecting LGBTQ+ Americans is not just a good social policy, it is good for the economy too. Car loans, a mortgage, student loans, and even small business loans can still be denied to members of the community without the Equality Act. This means we are impeding the economic growth and potential of our local communities, cities, states, and even the nation at large by choosing to discriminate. The Human Rights

Campaigns *"Business Coalition for the Equality Act"* is a list of leading US companies that support an end to discrimination policies. Together, these companies employ over 14.8 million workers across all fifty states and have a combined revenue of over seven trillion dollars (HRC, 2021). Apple, Amazon, Facebook, and Nike are among the companies that span the gamete from tech industry giants to the country's largest financial service providers, who all openly support the Equality Act.

America can no longer sit idly waiting for the right time to protect vulnerable communities. The LGBTQ+ community lives in fear every day under an administration that has not just attacked but failed to recognize the existence and importance of their community. Americans can't keep waiting and hoping that times will change and that the next election will bring the leaders we need. Though we may not always have allies in the Oval, we have allies in the Senate and even more in the House of Representatives.

Our time is now.

It is time that our elected officials show up and speak out for all of their constituents. It is time for clear and consistent protections under federal civil rights law. It is time for Equality.

PART II

THE SCIENCE OF QUEER RESILIENCE

6

A Ted Talk on Resilience

———

Adversity doesn't discriminate. If you're reading this, especially as a member of the broad queer community, you have likely already faced discrimination, adversity, setbacks, and direct questioning of your existence. Repeatedly, we have to defend our existence in a world that is not yet ready; a world where the norms include catastrophic gender reveals that focus on the binary interpretations and heteronormative constructions of sexuality. Children are born and presented to the world as "straight." Only if and when that child realizes they don't fit the norm established by society through religious suppression and cultural constructions of gender roles do they have to "come out."

A straight individual never has to defend their sexuality or gender identity. At what point does a hetero, cisgender man come out and say, "I'm straight and I love women!" Never. No one ever goes up to a hetero, cisgender man and asks them, "but are you sure you're straight? When did you know you were straight? How do you know if you have never been in a relationship with men?" Heterosexual, cisgender individuals get to go through life living their true, authentic selves without the anxiety of discrimination, without the need to defend themselves, without the fear of death based on their sexual orientation or gender identity. It is this comfort, this ability to live freely since their first breath, which limits and delays the development of resilience and leadership.

Everyone can develop resilience and leadership skills; this isn't something reserved for the LGBTQ+ community. What is different, however, is the speed with which these are galvanized into our being and when, in our development, the skills of resilience and leadership become a permanent part of our conscious toolkit. We learn from an early age that life isn't perfect and that it is not going to be easy. While growing up wealthy or white can make life easier, regardless of your sexuality or gender identity, you still face adversity, and your life will never be as easy, even though it may be similar to someone who isn't LGBTQ+. Yet somehow because of this insight, we can move on and turn the page with relative ease.

LIVED RESILIENCE

Speaking from first-hand experience, I know that other marginalized identities experience similar opportunities to find and harness their resilience and leadership skills. As a first-generation immigrant who grew up in a low-income household, I faced a unique set of challenges in addition to those I brought along with me because I struggled to understand my sexual orientation. I relied on the resilience I built through my struggle as a Mexican growing up in Texas in the early 2000s.

Xenophobia was everywhere, like a shadow that permanently followed me through my childhood. No matter where I went, I heard comments like "if one Mexican fails (referring to all of the Latinos in the classroom regardless of their ancestry), then none of you deserve to pass the class." I constantly heard "we don't speak Spanish in this country" or "you're not allowed to speak that language here," starting with my second-grade teacher all the way to my high junior year English teacher. It was as if the ability to cope with two languages crashing through my brain, like waves exploding onto the coast, was something to be made fun of instead of something in which to take pride.

My immigrant identity was what first gave me the ability to develop my resilience. I grew up thinking I was only Mexican until, one day, lawyers informed my family that I was born with dual nationality since my dad had been born in the United States. Suddenly, two teenagers found themselves with a child and, at no fault to them, the concept of citizenship was not a priority. I had realized this identity was the reason why I had developed the strength to rise from the ashes again and again, as if I was some sort of Mexican phoenix, regardless of the obstacles placed in my way. When I discovered that I was privileged enough (and not a day goes by that I am not aware of how fortunate I am) to be born with dual citizenship and had always had the same legal status as a natural-born citizen, my perspective shifted. Instead of gaining an identity, I lost both. I was confused and instantly felt like I didn't belong in Mexico or the United States.

My family had made the difficult choice to immigrate to the United States because my parents realized, even at their young age, that Mexico could not provide their growing family with the tools they needed to succeed. At that moment you feel rejected by your country of birth, by the country your family has history and pride in. Mexico, and many Mexicans, see you as a traitor for turning your back on your people to go north. Once you make it north, the United States sees you as a foreigner and collectively as an outsider who, for whatever reason, has come here. This is the story for many immigrants. We are no longer from there, but not accepted as being from here, and the older you are when you come to the United States the longer it takes for you to find that balance.

I was fortunate to move to the US at a young age and I am a proud, first-generation, gay, Mexican American. I am proud to struggle every single day to sort through my bilingual dictionary of words and phrases to find the exact one through which I can express myself. Because of these intersections of culture, language, and identity, I am here, I am queer, and I am resilient.

A TED TALK ON RESILIENCE

The formal study of resilience is done through the lens of childhood development or psychological evaluation. When you consider this in the development and psyche of LGBTQ+ individuals, there is something unique about our approach to resilience that is now being harnessed for us to take the next step and not just survive but become leaders. I am a firm believer that my leadership ability and that of other LGBTQ+ leaders around the world, is brought to the forefront because of our sexual orientation and/or gender identity. Being Latino and growing up low income formed my foundation and my values, more than my ability to be resilient.

Hindsight really is twenty-twenty. Now I realize how my life in the closet, my coming out process, and now living authentically, have fortified my sense of resilience and unleashed my leadership potential. The opportunity and ability to lead is always there within us, but the unique experiences lived by the LGBTQ+ community are the catalyst in unbridling, harnessing, and using our queer advantage to become effective leaders for all.

I know this is true because I am a leader within the LGBTQ+ community. I know this is true because I see it in my community. I am an expert in this because of my lived experiences, but academic and professional experts in leadership and resilience see it too. I am just here to connect the dots for you.

In a Ted Talk by Dr. Lucy Hone, a resilience expert and researcher, she describes the three secrets of resilient people. They understand that suffering is part of life, they carefully choose where to direct their attention, and they reflect. This set of skills are so obviously present within the LGBTQ+ community that you could replace "resilient people" in her talk with "queer people," and you wouldn't notice the difference. Mind-blowingly obvious when you're on the "inside" looking out, but when you're not from the queer community, when you're heterosexual and cisgender looking in, you are distracted by the glitter, captivated by the pride, and overwhelmed by your own sense of curiosity.

"SHIT HAPPENS"

"Resilient people get that shit happens. They know that suffering is part of life. This doesn't mean they welcome it in, they're not delusional. Just that when tough times come, they seem to know that suffering is part of every human existence" (Hone, 2019). Very much in line with Buddhist mentality and the core belief that all life is suffering known as Dukkha. "Knowing this stops you from feeling discriminated against when the tough times come" (Hone, 2020). History shows that the LGBTQ+ community is no stranger to suffering.

It is not that our community has become so accustomed to experiencing suffering and discrimination that we ignore it. It's just that through years of repeated verbal, physical, and mental attacks, by both society and ourselves, we have had no choice but to exercise the resiliency muscle in our brain to survive. Imagine having to carry all this emotional baggage with us throughout life. "Being resilient means you face stressors, not eliminate them. To be resilient means you learn from your mistakes, not avoid making them. To be resilient means you rebound from failure" says Raphael Rose, a Clinical Psychologist at UCLA (Rose, 2018).

Have you ever thrown an insult at an LGBTQ+ person? You are probably saying to yourself—"Well I haven't, but I know someone that has." I'm not here to judge. For those of you who have seen it happen in person or in film, have you noticed how quickly and with what technique LGBTQ+ people not only recover, but are prepared with a comeback? What many see in media, the over-stereotyped LGBTQ+ person, is nothing more than a defense mechanism developed through years of bullying and constant recognition that shit does happen and you might as well be ready for it.

PICK WISELY

"Resilient people are really good at choosing carefully where they select their attention. They have a habit of realistically appraising situations, and typically, managing to focus on the things that they can change, and somehow accept the things that they can't." This, Dr. Hone asserts is a "vital, learnable skill for resilience" (Hone, 2020).

Dr. Hone describes how "as humans, we are good at noticing threats and weaknesses. We are hardwired for that negative. We're really, really good at noticing them. Negative emotions stick to us like Velcro, whereas positive emotions and experiences seem to bounce off like Teflon" (Hone, 2020). This is one of the resilience traits that the LGBTQ+ community develops quickly, early on in life. We carefully choose where to direct our attention. Much of this is learned early on while we are still in the closet making sure that our attention signals to the world "we are straight." Depending on our situation, this attention might be directed towards protecting and defending ourselves once we are out.

While it may be a part of what makes LGBTQ+ people resilient, this constant need to redirect attention can have some negative effects. Serious mental illness among LGBTQ+ populations has significantly increased since 2015. There was an average increase of one hundred thousand individuals ages eighteen to twenty-five, and double that per year for those ages twenty-six to forty-nine, according to the 2019 National

Survey on Drug Use and Health, by the Substance Abuse and Mental Health Services Administration. Still, Dr. Rose says that "even undesirable outcomes provide the opportunity to better rebound and recover from stress and promote resilience" (Rose, 2018).

Broadly today, according to Dr. Hone, "the problem is, we now live in an era where we are constantly bombarded by threats all day long, and our poor brains treat every single one of those threats as though they were a tiger. Our threat focus, our stress response, is permanently dialed up. Resilient people don't diminish the negative, but they also have worked out a way of tuning into the good" (Hone, 2020). Dr. Rose from UCLA agrees that resilient individuals are more likely to experience positive emotions rather than negative ones. Now I don't know the percentage of positive versus negative emotions experienced by LGBTQ+ individuals, but I will make the bold claim that we feel those emotions, especially the positive emotions, on a deeper and more intense level. We know how to create spaces where you truly feel euphoria.

Have you ever been to a gay nightclub? I'm not talking about just a gay bar with music, but a gay nightclub, one of those that doesn't close until four in the morning, and where people don't actually arrive until after midnight. Come to think of it, we should call it a morning club, but that's a conversation for another time. A nightclub where the music is loud enough to make you literally feel it, but also make you feel like you might as well be the only one there listening with noise-canceling headphones. In this type of music, at just the right level where the rest of the world disappears, a beat consumes you. Here, the lights cast just the right glow on the crowd of bodies swaying to the beat. The lights change colors with the music, but you feel they are connected to the emotions that the chorus of *"Dancing Queen"* makes you feel. Nothing compares to the euphoria generated by a gay nightclub regardless of whether it is in Paris, New York, or the outskirts of Cancun.

MIRROR MIRROR

Lastly, Dr. Hones says that "resilient people ask themselves 'is what I'm doing helping or harming me?'" She says that this is an important aspect of building resilience because it allows you to control your decisions and check-in with yourself. Speaking from personal experience here, I don't know if I checked in with myself the time I chose to dye my hair platinum blond one holiday before traveling to Morocco—did I enjoy it? Yes. Did it help or hurt me while two gay men were traveling through the medina of Marrakech? The verdict is still out on that one. What I do know is that having the ability to check in with yourself, know why you're taking an action, and being able to advocate for yourself and your decision, is one of the greatest lessons I have recently learned. There was no course in college or even graduate school to help me develop this skill. What I knew is that I didn't want my race, gender, sexual orientation, or socioeconomic background to be someone else's excuse for why I made a decision or took a stance. I wanted to be able to back these decisions on merit, knowledge, and yes, even experience, but never under the premise that one of my identities could place blinders on my decision-making progress.

In summary, Dr. Hones shares that the secret of resilient people are that they realize that life is, well, complicated, but choose to focus on the positive rather than the negative, and they also check in with themselves to have honest conversations. Dr. Rose expands this by adding that resilient individuals are open to new experiences and embrace challenges, are socially connected, and truly believe that their network is their net worth. They also "engage in something meaningful for the joy it brings" (Rose, 2018), not just to be a part of it.

RINSE AND REPEAT

Dr. Rose also highlights the importance of slow and gradual change as better than a one-off moment or pressured behavior change (Rose, 2018). Gradual change and growth is at the center of the LGBTQ+ community. Things are gradual, either by choice or by necessity. In so many ways, we test the waters before coming out. We don't have a unique, patented way to figure out if someone we like also likes us. Yes, there are certain places where the chances are almost 99 percent that the other person identifies how we do, but we can't straight-up hit on a barista or a cashier. I mean, yes we can, but the chances that the person reciprocates positively are slim. These types of encounters can end up violent or even deadly depending on how the other party takes it. We must be gradual, calculated, and think things through about our technique, especially in public. Each one of these encounters makes us more resilient.

Even after we come out, the process is still gradual. Once we are out and proud about who we are, there are still so many barriers and obstacles to overcome from within the LGBTQ+ community. The grass isn't greener on the other side, but at least there aren't any fences. There is an entire culture, language, and even belief system depending on how you identify. While Beyonce, Madonna, and Lady Gaga may simply be artists to some, they are borderline deities within the LGBTQ+ community, and these are just the megastars cisgender straight people know about. There could be a whole study, a whole book on the close to cult followings of actual queer artists like Janelle Monàe, Kim Petras, Troy Sivan, Hayley Kioko, Ricky Martin, and Rina Sawayama. These are crucial pieces of knowledge you learn in "You're Queer 101" and the "Music for your next Kiki 347" in order to get your "gay card." I have mine laminated.

The LGBTQ+ community is here, contrary to popular belief, and for a long time, not just a good time. Marriage equality took decades of work, and the struggle for equality at all levels of society continues to this very day. In 2021, the LGBTQ+ population made up almost 6 percent of the US population, yet we aren't even 2 percent of all elected officials, at all levels, much less Congress (Jones, 2021). We continue to weather the storm in the hopes of one day seeing the rainbow of equality proudly stretch from sea to shining sea.

Ultimately the wide and diverse queer community is uniquely poised to not just develop the skills needed to become resilient at a very early age but reinforce and perfect them throughout life. Being one of us isn't a defect. It isn't a setback. It's an advantage. It means being born with the incredible potential to create meaningful and long-lasting positive change wherever we happen to be. As we build the courage to come out, we come out not at a disadvantage, but with the incredible capability to be resilient and become the leaders we need today.

BUILDING LEADERSHIP

The thing about queer, resilient leadership is that you can't learn it, you can only live it. There are hundreds, maybe even thousands of leadership development programs and courses in the United States alone for every identity and interest out there. While many of these dive deep into the nuances of various intersections, there are some shared characteristics of what makes one a leader for today's world. Leadership Expert Roselinde Torres, a Senior Partner and Managing Director at the Boston Consulting Group's People and Organization practice area, shares three questions that twenty-first-century leaders must be able to answer if they want to lead in her TED Talk. The first two are

1. Where are you looking to anticipate change?
2. What is the diversity measure of your professional and personal network?

These first two are part of either a skillset or resource bank that anyone can develop over time. You can pick up a new habit, take a course, and develop the ability, as Roselinde puts it, to "shape the future rather than just react. To be able to look around corners" (Torres, 2013). Building a diverse network takes more time and energy. You must be able to develop the ability to maintain and develop authentic connections based on trust and respect. In the end, "having a more diverse network is a greater source of pattern identification and leads to greater solutions" (Torres, 2013).

However, the third question posed by Roselinde is harder to answer.

3. Are you courageous enough to abandon the past and pave a new path?

You need to almost be born with the capability to answer the third one—queer people most certainly are. This isn't to say that you can't develop the courage and strength to reject standards and norms, but when these standards and heterosexual norms have benefited you and your views of the world, would you be so quick to reject them in order to lay the first brick down for the benefit of all? Do you see "that quiet isn't always peace and the norms and notions of what is just, isn't always justice" (Gorman, 2021)?

These new leaders, these queer leaders, have built the emotional stamina to withstand the hate hurled hastily and with hurricane-like force at our community. Still, see something salvageable in society. Queer, resilient leaders lead in multiple ways. We lead through merit, with transparency, and with honesty. We lead through empathy and community. We lead because we are compelled to do so. If great leaders dare to be different and take risks, then queer leaders are here like the superheroes our societies around the world need today, more than ever, if we are to break past the binary and see the full spectrum of color.

7

Leading with Merit

———

LGBTQ+ leaders across the country don't go into the office with the goal of only advancing the gay agenda – maybe this is what makes them so intimidating. They must overcome multiple, incredible obstacles just to be on the ballot, and then struggle with winning over voters. Once they are in office, once they have learned all the lessons that come from facing constant rejection and homophobia, they win their race and go into their elected office with a tremendous level of resilience incomparable to any other candidate.

You've probably heard of Harvey Milk. If the name triggered some sort of thought process leading towards the conclusion that Harvey Milk must have something to do with the milk industry, even the plant-based one, then I don't blame you. Instead, I blame our underfunded education system that doesn't do enough to teach queer history or that of any other minority and marginalized group for that matter. Now, do you know who Kathy Kozachenko is? Nope, not a Russian spy during the Cold War, but the first openly LGBTQ+ person ever elected in the United States. Though she was the first, she will not be the last.

SHATTERING THE GLASS CEILING

Kathy Kozachenko is not a common household name despite her ceiling-shattering election, a win for the LGBTQ+ community. Originally from Alexandria, Virginia, she ran for a local city council office in Ann Arbor, Michigan. Adding to the historical nature of her candidacy and election, she ran as neither a member of the Republican nor Democratic party, but as a member of the Human Rights Party. Despite being a third party, the Human Rights Party had already had success in Michigan politics, having won two seats previously and both held by LGBTQ+ members who came out during their term in office instead of before their election, creating a certain precedent for Kozachenko's run. In April of 1974, she won her election, making history as the first 'out' elected individual in the United States. However, it seemed that the policies of the Human Rights Party, and the liberal policies of Ann Arbor, took center stage in the article run by *The Michigan Daily* about Kozachenko's election, instead of the historic nature of her win (Fries, 2015).

So why is it that we don't hear more about Kathy Kozachenko's historic race, yet there was a film made about Harvey Milk? In an interview with the Victory Institute Kozachenko says, "I didn't set out to make history. When I first ran for office in 1974 as an openly lesbian candidate, I ran to promote the social justice policies of the Human Rights Party, which included pro-feminist and pro-LGBTQ+ stances in addition to an unwavering commitment to economic and racial justice. I ran in a Michigan college town, in a college ward, where being a lesbian wasn't entirely disqualifying."

Though she does mention the significance of her run, Kozachenko reinforces the significance that her success came through being a third-party candidate. Kozachenko, who was an English major at the University of Michigan, is described by those who know her as a poet at heart who found herself wrapped up in politics not because she sought public service as a career, but because she wanted to increase rights for all.

Kozachenko eventually left politics and did not run for a second term, but that's not to say she left advocacy. She continued to advocate for farm and union workers. In doing this work, she met MaryAnn Geiger. The two eventually went on to create a family together with MaryAnn's four children from a prior marriage and a child they had together. Kozachenko's advocacy and historic nature took a backseat towards her newly established family. Yes, it was the 1970s, but up until 2020, there were no explicit federal protections for LGBTQ+ individuals stating that you could not be fired for being queer (Totenberg, 2020). So instead of preaching to the masses that she was the first LGBTQ+ candidate elected in the United States, she worked and focused on her new career and on being a mother. We still, unjustly so, often ask strong pioneering women to take a back seat from their careers to be moms.

Kathy Kozachenko was followed by Elaine Noble, the first LGBTQ+ candidate elected to a state legislature in 1974, who served two terms in Massachusetts State Legislature (Ginaulis, 2015). Bet you didn't know that name right off the top of your head. Contrary to more recent elected officials from the community Elaine Noble shared in an interview that she viewed her election as "being elected in spite of being gay, not because of it." Even though her election was in the greater Boston area, a liberal stronghold now for many years, she describes her campaign as 'ugly.' There was a lot of shooting through my windows, destroying my car, breaking windows at [her] campaign headquarters, serious harassment of people visiting my house and campaign office—it was really bad" (Schlittler, 2009). She later ran, unsuccessfully, for the Democratic nomination for US Senator and later worked for the Office of the Mayor of Boston, Kevin White, before going into healthcare consulting.

Two women came before Harvey Milk's election. Two women whose names are not at the tip of the tongue for future leaders. These two women paved the way for the LGBTQ+ community, who seem to have been forgotten in our collective history, and they are two white women. How many women of color exist whose history and contributions we are unaware?

THE MAYOR OF CASTRO

Harvey Milk doesn't even get the title of the first gay man elected to public office in the United States. That historic first goes to Jim Yeadon. In 1976, he was elected to the City Council of Madison Wisconsin at the age of twenty-six (Schwamb, 2007). By the time he was elected, there were already a handful of women who were out and serving at various levels across the country. Kozachenko, Yeadon, and Noble shared many things in common. They were all under the age of thirty when elected to office, so don't let anyone tell you you're too young to run for office. Both Kozachenko and Yeadon served in City Council first, as did many of the early LGBTQ+ elected officials. This cemented the idea that election matters, not just the election that determines who lives at 1600 Pennsylvania Avenue.

So why do we know so much about Harvey Milk? Yes, he was also a historic first. He was the first openly LGBTQ+ person elected to office in the state of California and eventually the first openly gay city commissioner in the United States ("The Official Harvey Milk Biography"). Unlike Kozachenko, Noble, and Yeadon, Milk was the first LGBTQ+ elected official, and possibly the only one, to be murdered while in office. In 1977, after three failed attempts to win an elected office, he became a member of the San Francisco Board of Supervisors. He was sworn in January 1978 and assassinated in November 1978 by a former member of the Board of Supervisors, Dan White, who also killed Mayor George Moscone that night.

Unlike previous candidates, Harvey was one of the first LGBTQ+ candidates who not only leaned on his sexuality but also used it to build support from the wider LGBTQ+ community. Other candidates before him had not necessarily hidden their sexuality from their voters, as previously described, and felt that they won their elections despite being LGBTQ+ not because of it.

Harvey's 1977 run wasn't his first attempt at running for office, and by this time he had learned how to activate the community in support for one of their own. However, he was a pioneer in the world of LGBTQ+ business, an area for which he is less known than his political activism. When he came to San Francisco in 1972, he opened a camera store in what is now the Castro District, or the gay village of San Francisco (Milk Foundation).

As a small business owner, he faced the common challenges of any up-and-coming business regardless of his sexuality. It takes a tremendous amount of resilience as is to open a business in the first place. As Castro Street grew and took shape into the gay-friendly area many of us know it for today, there were individual businesses that attempted to slow down its gayification. Harvey founded the Castro Village Association, essentially a Business Improvement District (BID), focused on the economic development and well-being of the Castro. Different from most BIDs of their time, this one was comprised predominantly of LGBTQ+ businesses, and Milk was elected president, giving him the ability to be the face of the economic empowerment of the LGBTQ+ business in the area. This, combined with his prior experience and exposure running for office, helped him secure a win in 1977.

After all the struggles and discriminations for being gay, Harvey served not just the gay community of the Castro, but all of San Francisco, regardless of their sexuality. Yes, he went in intending to defend and protect gay rights, sponsoring an anti-discrimination bill which was one of the most progressive bills of its time (Ledbetter, 1978), but He also drew national support to fight against Proposition six (Ring, 2018), which sought to legalize discrimination against the LGBTQ+ community. Harvey also advocated for tax code reform that would boost industry, the creation of low-income housing by repurposing unused military facilities, and establishing childcare services for working moms (Onion, Sullivan, Mullen, 2017).

Aside from his horrific death, Harvey was a talented speaker, and the Harvey Milk Foundation aids our collective ability to remember his presence. On coming out, Milk said, "gay people, we will not win our rights by staying quietly in our closets. ... We are coming out to fight the lies, the myths, the distortions. We are coming out to tell the truths about gays, for I am tired of the conspiracy of silence, so I'm going to talk about it. And I want you to talk about it. You must come out" (Milk Foundation).

This sentiment still rings true and strong today. Those of us fortunate enough to come out do so not just for ourselves, but with the obligation that we must be ready to fight for our rights and community at a moment's notice. Harvey Milk also seemed to know that while coming out gives you a great sense of pride and purpose, it perpetually puts a rainbow target on your back. In preparation for the unthinkable, he famously recorded as part of his will, "If a bullet should enter [his] brain, let that bullet destroy every closet door" ("The Official Harvey Milk Biography").

BECAUSE OF, NEVER DESPITE

Harvey's experiences as a member of a targeted and marginalized community, combined with his resilience to get up after defeat, made him a strong member on the Board of Supervisors. All LGBTQ+ community leaders, from Kozachenko to Mondaire Jones, have gone into office ready to advocate for every single member of their community regardless of if they voted for them or not. From the beginning of our presence on the political stage, we have advocated for the wider breadth of the community which we are a part of, not just those who are queer. Equally, we are bold enough to go into office not just to advance the gay agenda, but to engage in a wide set of policies.

It does seem that, as a community, we gravitate towards transportation policy as our area of focus. This seems to also be the subject area in which we are uniquely qualified to serve. No, I am not talking about Secretary of Transportation Pete Buttigieg, I am talking about the historic election of Danica Roem. Danica Roem was the first openly transgender person elected to a state legislature, representing the 13th District of Virginia to the General Assembly.

Delegate Roem's website makes it very clear "If you followed my 2017 campaign, you may have seen my 'Fix Route 28 Now!' yard signs. If you followed my career as your local news reporter at the Gainesville Times from 2006-2015, you know I often took deep dives into transportation policy." Transportation isn't her only priority for those in the thirteenth District, or the Virginias across the entire Commonwealth. Education, transparency and accountability, health care, environment, gun violence prevention, equity, equality, inclusion, and tax policies have all been areas of focus for the delegate since first winning her election in 2017.

Before public service, Roem' spent over ten years as a reporter which gave her the skills to "listen to what people were saying and understand their reasoning, regardless of [her] opinions" (Roem). She goes further to say that her job as an "elected representative isn't to speak. It is to listen to the residents, write down their concerns, ideas, and questions, follow-up with them, and work what they tell [her] into [her] policy platform." You actually won't find any mention of her sexuality or gender on her website. It's focused on policy, skills, and the ability to serve her constituents. This in no way means that she isn't proud of who she is, but she is just as proud to be a stepmom and a self-described metal-head.

There are no words to describe the feeling I had when I first met Danica Roem. I was in my first semester of graduate school back at Georgetown. Running point on all things advocacy I, along with three other students, established the McCourt LGBTQ+ Policy Initiative (LPI). Using the platform of LPI, along with other key organizations on campus, we invited Delegate Roem to come to speak. She was incredible. Honest, transparent, funny, and undisputedly resilient. After all, she had just unseated a homophobic Republican who had held the delegate seat for over two decades. She spoke with an incredible amount of passion and knowledge about the people of the thirteenth district and their needs. If it wasn't because the event was mainly sponsored by a Catholic university's LGBTQ+ organizations, you might have thought we were all there to listen to either a very funny transportation wonk or a stand-up comedian whose material was focused on transportation jokes. Yet, it was a full house to listen to a delegate speak about her story.

I ran into Delegate Roem a few months later at a major fundraising event for the LGBTQ+ Victory Fund while I was interning for the Victory Institute, "the only national organization dedicated to elevating openly LGBTQ+ leaders at all levels of government." I would later have the incredible honor to join their team in 2020 as the presidential appointments manager, a position through which I get to truly make the "by the people, for the people" idea of America happen, ensuring representation at all levels of the administration. I never actually went up to talk to Roem at this event. Instead, I lingered. Even if I was an "old" intern, I was still the intern back then, and there for work, not to get starstruck by an elected official.

Our paths did cross again, in early 2020, at the Blue Commonwealth Gala a month before restrictions were set across the United States due to COVID-19. By this point, I had begun to take the plunge into state politics, joining various Democratic organizations across the Commonwealth, mainly the official Latino Caucus of the Democratic Party of Virginia, an organization I had the honor to be elected to lead in 2021. Through my involvement in DLOV, and my incredible mentor, I was invited to attend this gala. This was the first time this gay immigrant, first-gen, double graduate was given the opportunity to attend an event like this and actually eat the food being served. Previously, I'd had to stand in the back and eat a boxed lunch in another room because I was working the event as part of an internship or as a volunteer.

With the help of a friend, I built up the courage to approach Delegate Roem. I didn't want to speak to her or ask her for anything, I just wanted to thank her for paving the path for others to follow. I was so nervous, and my palms were probably sweating. (Roem, if you're ever reading this, I'm sorry for what was likely a very sweaty handshake.) I opened my mouth and impostor syndrome immediately kicked in. I felt like I didn't belong in that room and felt like I was once again a volunteer or intern who shouldn't be in the same room as these elected officials. I would be lying to you if I told you that I said this or that to Delegate Roem, but I do remember messing up. My feelings of "you don't belong here" and "you're wasting her time" kicked in and in whatever I said I used the word "despite."

If you know Delegate Roem, then you know that her response was "never despite, but because of our identity. I'm here, and I'm unapologetically here, and I want you to know you can succeed because of who you are." Those words have stuck with me, and are repeated *ad nauseam* throughout this book, and I try my best to remember that I am where I am because of who I am, not despite it.

"Because of, never despite." This is powerful.

Members of the LGBTQ+ community are meant to run and win elected offices because they are qualified, not despite their sexual orientation or gender identity. Instead of getting mad, Danica, Pete, Kathy, Elaine, and Harvey all got elected and used their merit to truly win the hearts and minds, of their voters.

8

Leading First and Foremost

———

For over 20 years of my life, I wasn't gay. Well, you know what I mean, I wasn't out… not even to myself. I lived a tremendous part of my life, some would even argue the most critical years of my life, in the closet. When I finally did come out, I spent so much of that time convincing people that nothing had changed and that I was still the same Jonathan, regardless of my sexuality. I still haven't completely decompressed that excuse because while in oh-so-many ways my identity as a gay man did not change a thing, other aspects of me ceased to exist the day I came out.

For starters, I no longer had to pretend to both myself and others that I was someone I wasn't. I had fit so many of the gay stereotypes for so much of my life, for better or for worse, but I had fought hard for people to see me as something other than "just gay." I wanted to be invisible. I wanted to blend in, which often meant trying desperately, and failing with the same level of intensity, to be seen as straight. I had managed to convince *myself* that I was straight, so much so that I would get defensive and maybe even angry when my façade was questioned. This seldom worked, and it probably dragged more attention to my sexuality.

I am incredibly proud and loud about my sexuality, but it is not something I announce to every person I meet. I don't go around introducing myself by saying "Hi, my name is Jonathan Dromgoole and I am gay." I also don't do a single thing in the world to hide my sexuality. Authenticity has become such a big part of my life since coming out. It is probably one of the biggest changes, along with my overall happiness, that took place when I came out to myself on the steps of the Paris Opera and then publicly, for the first time, to my friend Rachel. There was an immediate need to never go back into the closet, to make sure that those doors were blown off the hinges and make sure that I was who I was always meant to be.

Even though the need to come out was so intense that it eventually led me to say, "I'm gay," that same feeling felt like an obligation, not to someone else, but to myself to constantly come out. It became a burden, a weight to carry, and I didn't want to be seen as "just that gay kid." After spending so many years of my life as someone else, with a fake sense of identity, I didn't want to have to now depend on my true identity as some sort of crutch to carry me throughout life. Yes, I'm gay, but that's not all that I am. At some point in my coming out process, I stopped coming out, I stopped announcing my presence, and I simply took a deep breath and lived.

THE RAINBOW APPLE

"We pave the sunlit path towards justice together, brick by brick. This is my brick." – Tim Cook (Cook, 2014).

Coming out, regardless of your situation, can be a frightening moment in your life. Not only does this moment critically mark your life with a clear "before and after," but it simultaneously opens you up in the most intimate ways possible. Imagine coming out in your late fifties while you're running a business. Seems intense right? How difficult must it be to spend most of your life publicly in the closet with only those closest to you knowing who you truly are? I spent twenty-one years in the closet and let me tell you, that was rough. Now imagine if that business you oversaw was none other than Apple.

Tim Cook was named CEO of Apple in August of 2011, when its pioneering founder Steve Jobs resigned as CEO, after repeatedly struggling with his health and battle with cancer, to focus on his role as chairman of the board of directors (Arthur, 2011). Unlike Steve Jobs, Tim Cook is not synonymous with Apple or a black turtleneck, but he is no less important. Though Tim Cook may have been a relatively new name, and in 2011 still under the shadow of Jobs, he was in no way a newcomer to Apple. Since 1998, Cook has been a key part of turning Apple around and most recently served as the chief operating officer for the tech giant, focusing on global sales and operations and management of Apple's global supply chain, sales, and services (Apple, 2021). Six weeks after Cook's appointment as CEO, Steve Jobs passed away, leaving Tim in control of a company without its visionary founder (Markoff, 2011).

Without Cook, Apple could not have developed into the global powerhouse we seem to assume it has always been. When Cook joined Apple, his goal was to turn around a failing business model that had become too expensive to sustain. In three years, Apple's revenue had plummeted from eleven billion dollars in 1995 to six billion in 1998 (Nicas, 2018). Needless to say, and hard to believe especially now with revenue over $274 billion twenty-five years later, that Apple was going nowhere and very fast (Apple, 2021).

It is hard to imagine a world without Apple. Yes, I am sure the technology would still exist, but would we want it in the same way we want an Apple product? The way the products and the brand speak to consumers, in this age of mass consumerism, promotes a sense of exclusivity, individuality, and freedom. The first Apple product I ever owned was a bright metallic blue iPod Shuffle —

second generation—for my thirteenth birthday in 2007. Picture me with blond highlights, a purple polo, and holding the box with the blue iPod Shuffle while staring at the camera; yup definitely "not gay" back then. With a retail price of one hundred and fifty dollars, this was not easily attainable for my family back in 2007, but the idea that you could show your personality not only through the music you had on your iPod, but the color of it, gave Apple a welcoming sense of inclusivity, individuality, and freedom.

This seems to be ingrained into the fabric of the tech giant, and for many of Apple's LGBTQ+ customers, we feel the power of this movement despite it not necessarily spending advertising dollars on us (Stiffler, 2019). However, Apple's decision to be more inclusive may have been just as strategic and thought out as Tim Cook's decision to publicly come out in 2014.

In October of 2014, Tim Cook came out in a very public, yet tech industry-specific, manner—through a letter published on Bloomberg's website. Since joining Apple, Cook had often taken a back seat and remained fairly private about his personal life. In his coming out announcement, he wrote, "throughout my professional life, I've tried to maintain a basic level of privacy. I come from humble roots, and I don't seek to draw attention to myself." There are reports that he even used a different gym from the rest of his employees. This makes the public online announcement of his sexuality seem more in line with today's social media influences, rather than our preconceived notions of the stereotypical CEO.

Is there a right way to come out? No. There is a perfect way though, your way, whatever that might be.

In a very Tim Cook fashion, he put the needs of Apple before his own needs. Leaders within the LGBTQ+ community are experts at prioritizing others, but especially their business, career, or education, before their personal goals. We spend so much time in the closet hiding our sexuality from the world that we must, or at least often, come up with clever nuggets of gold to sprinkle around. This is a defense mechanism intended to distract even our closest friends from prying into our personal life. As these nuggets catch on, we nurture them. They grow and we become them. We become the accomplished artist staring in the school play, the president of an honor society or student body, or the first in our family to go to college. Our identity becomes these nuggets of academic and professional success. We prioritize these needs, knowing there will be a high return on investment later on in our lives... at least we hope so.

By coming out in October of 2014, Cook had already prioritized Apple's yearly September announcement of new products, software, and gadgets. He put Apple, its profits, and ultimately the needs of the investors ahead of his own. In his Op-ed he wrote that "Apple is already one of the most closely watched companies in the world, and [he] like[s] keeping the focus on [their] products and the incredible things [their] customers achieve with them." Business is synonymous with profits, not with individual freedoms, and to stay at the top requires a certain level of resilience. Much in the same way that an individual must come out time and again and see if it is safe to do so, a company embracing the LGBTQ+ also must come out and test the corporate waters. By publicly coming out, Tim Cook became the first openly gay CEO of not just a *Fortune Top Ten*, but a *Fortune 500* company in 2014.

There was no corporate handbook or guide to instruct him on how to navigate the dangerous corporate waters where CEOs are voted out by their boards left and right. I mean they don't call it *Shark Tank* for nothing. However, Cook says that coming out has "also given [him] the skin of a rhinoceros, which comes in handy when you're the CEO of Apple" (Cook, 2014). His queer identity, and not the industry titles, gave him the resilience to survive in such a competitive, corporate climate, and is likely what has made him a successful CEO.

Despite the potential risks associated with coming out in such a public manner, Tim Cook considers that "being gay is not a limitation. It's a feature." When discussing the advantages of being gay, Cook explains that it "has given me a deeper understating of what it means to be in the minority and provide a window into the challenges that people in other minority groups deal with every day." In a way, this is what gives our community a sense of identity—a shared knowledge of the challenges we have faced and continue to face in our everyday lives. Being a member of this community makes us "more empathetic, which [leads] to a richer life. It's tough and uncomfortable at times, but it [gives us] the confidence to be [ourselves], to follow [our] own path, and to rise above adversity and bigotry," as Cook shared in his Bloomberg letter.

Though the shift in the culture of the mega-brand is in no small way due to the shift at the top, Tim Cook's decision to share something so private in such a public manner was not so he could push the gay agenda, as some conspiracy theories that are likely floating around may want us to believe. For many of us, especially those within the LGBTQ+ community, Cook's time at the helm of the powerhouse company has brought on a sense of inclusivity, acceptance, and visibility. Over his term as CEO, Cook has used his platform to speak up for the entire community. As a gay, cisgender, white man, he has used his privilege to highlight the impacts of discrimination felt by members of the trans and non-binary community and has focused on advocating for LGBTQ+ youth.

At the same time, and very much in Cook's style, it has been at a gradual, yet consistent pace of representation, as if testing the waters with each increasingly queer release. Always a CEO first. In 2012 same-sex partner emojis were released, in 2015 they were expanded to include same-sex families, and in 2016 the pride flag was finally added as an emoji. Even though Cook came out in 2014, it wasn't until 2017 that Apple released its first Pride edition watch band and has subsequently done so in June of each year (Gil, 2020).

These have all been incremental yet extremely powerful changes for a brand with a global reach. A trans flag was finally added in 2020, but there are still no bisexual, lesbian, asexual, intersex, or pansexual pride flags (Baska, 20202). The more inclusive progress pride flag, which includes the colors of the trans flag as well as a brown and black stripe, is also missing, but over thirty emojis pop up if you type the word clock. The slow progress of inclusive emojis detracts from the contributions made by trans women of color in a community dominated by cisgender, white men. Bi-erasure, or the promoting the idea that bisexuality is simply an in-between being queer or being straight, unfortunately, remains present within the limited emoji keyboard.

If I were a betting man, I would say that even with all the advancements and strange emojis on the iPhone, the one thing Tim Cook uses the least is "find my friends" given how much he values his privacy. He is known to prefer to talk about Apple rather than his personal life and prefers to use an outside gym despite there being one on the Apple Campus (Cain, 2018). If he had already achieved professional success, valued his privacy, and was good at keeping his professional and personal life separate, then why come out in such a public manner and after so many years? Visibility.

At the end of the day, it is undeniable the cultural power and influence that comes with being the CEO of Apple. Tim could have just as easily kept his private life separate from the business. So why risk it all?

To quote Uncle Ben from Spiderman, "With great power, there must also come great responsibility" (Alves, 2020). Those fortunate and privileged enough within the queer community who can be out, have a shared sense of responsibility to be proud and visible. We do it not just for those who can't be safely and proudly themselves, but for the next generation growing up in a world that is not fully inclusive. As much as coming out may make our own lives better, the visibility gained from one more LGBTQ+ individual being out in the world can have a tremendous impact on those around us, regardless of if we are leaders among a group of friends or the CEO.

In deciding to come out, Cook shared that "it was my hope that pulling back the curtain on my own private life would help someone, anyone out there." He also considers "being gay among the greatest gifts God has given me," but at the same time does not consider himself "an activist, but I realize how much I have benefited from the sacrifice of others. So, if hearing that the CEO of Apple is gay can help someone struggling to come to terms with who they are, or bring comfort to anyone who feels alone, or inspires people to insist on their equality, then it's worth the trade-off with my own privacy."

We all share, to some extent, a common thread of lived experiences that automatically unite us. When we see a rainbow, whether it's a flag on a porch, a sticker on a water bottle, or a strap on a smartwatch, we see more than just a set of colors or a label. Quite literally, we see pride.

NOT TO PRIME IS A CRIME

With close to fourteen million followers, which is larger than the population of any US city, Nikkie de Jager, better known as Nikkie Tutorials, is one of the most popular beauty influencers on YouTube. "When I started my channel, I was fourteen years old and there was no money, there were no ads, so it truly started from passion and falling in love with the idea and that illusion of makeup," she says in her documentary *Layers of Me*. She grew up right on YouTube, creating a world where she could be whoever she wanted and for her, that was just Nikkie. Not Nikkie, the transgender beauty guru.

Social media does not give us the complete picture. Nikkie de Jager is well known within the beauty industry for her over-the-top, vibrant makeup. Her Halloween tutorials, welcoming personality, and Dutch word of the day at the end of all of her videos draw viewers to her. She has spent over thirteen years on YouTube building a brand focused on her skills as an artist, not on her gender.

Why would someone's gender identity have anything to do with makeup? What does it have to do with their careers? Unfortunately, perception.

Society attempts to pigeonhole LGBTQ+ individuals, but especially transgender individuals, as nothing more than their identity. We don't pursue jobs and dreams that are only for the queer community. Just look at Hollywood, they are casting and nominating actors left and right for portraying people from our community instead of nominating films by and for our community #DisclosureOscarSnub. It wasn't until January of 2020, over a decade after starting her channel, that de Jager came out to her fans as a transgender woman.

Nikkie de Jager is first and foremost a creative, an influencer, and a beauty icon, more so than she would likely say she is Dutch and about a hundred other things before labeling herself as a transgender woman. YouTube was a way of creating a safe space, a way of creating her world. In her documentary, she explains that "it wasn't until later, until it started growing [my channel and fame] that I was like, 'now there are a lot of people that don't know' and I really liked that idea. Now I get to be Nikkie without the past, the opinions, the side comments. YouTube let me be me without being misunderstood because they didn't know about that part. Is it lying? Yeah, but it's also protecting yourself."

Remember those nuggets of gold sprinkled around to distract friends and family? Those nuggets are there to protect us, the queer individuals, as much as they are there to distract others. Well, those nuggets can also be shared now, thanks to technology with a wider audience, to billions of people. At some point, as she explains, "You live your life the way you always wanted to live it, without getting judged for who you are, what you are, for what you were in the past, and you feel so free and so understood. You feel like you don't always have to talk about your past or about the thing that hurt you the most. And then you're like 'okay well apparently I get to live my life freely' so why would I bring all the pain back up?" Coming out time and time again is an exhausting process.

Sometimes it truly is easier to wear some sort of "pride" merchandise that will automatically signal to the world "hey I'm not straight" just so you don't have to have the potentially awkward, and in the worst-case dangerous, conversation with a friend or employer.

Bravely, de Jager shares her experience growing up knowing she was trans.

"Imagine you're a young kid and you find out about yourself, that you hate the body that you're in. You disgust yourself. Every day is a fight against yourself and your own body. Once you win that fight, it feels like we made it and then you make friends, and you're like, 'oh they know me for the person who I am not what I was' and I don't know if I am speaking for all transgender people, but at one point you want to close the chapter and let it be."

In a similar way to Tim Cook, and possibly to many LGBTQ+ leaders who became leaders before their identity became a defining force behind them, there was a moment where de Jager felt compelled to speak out. When an influencer, regardless of the industry, begins to notice just exactly who they are influencing and how much they mean to that often-marginalized community, something changes.

Despite neither Tim Cook nor Nikkie Tutorials hiding who they have always been from close friends and family, it takes a spark of a moment for them to see that they have the power to enact change.

For de Jager, it was a meet and greet in Kuwait City, Kuwait—a country where homosexuality is still illegal. A country in which Nikkie de Jager herself is considered illegal simply because of who she has always been. Security escorted men and boys out who had shown up to meet her. At an event where the focal point was a makeup beauty guru, their gender meant they could not be there. Cultural norms aside, the fact that their gender was in direct conflict with their passion, was something that made de Jager realize there was a community to fight for, a community that she belonged to despite never publicly acknowledging it.

Our identity is undeniably always present, even when we don't know who we are just yet. Even within the LGBTQ+ community, sometimes all we know is that the individual is just "not straight," but may not know how they truly identify. We may know they are married, how many pets they have, where they went to school, what they do for a living, etc. We may even know very personal and intimate details about another member of the community and yet still not know how they choose to identify. As a community, we can lead without the emphasis always being on our gender identity and sexual orientation. Some may feel they never need to come out in certain settings because some other aspect of who they are defines them in those spaces.

Coming out is something we, the community, do for ourselves and, in turn, choose to bring others into our lives and experiences. Coming out, even if it is just to ourselves, is critical. In many ways, it takes the weight off that allows us to focus and take care of our whole person. As time has progressed and we have achieved progress, we have seen how coming out has helped rather than hindered the careers of movers and shakers. At the same time, coming out after accomplishing great professional achievements illustrates that being queer doesn't change us. A person's sexual orientation or gender identity isn't a crutch to our achievements. It's not a crutch to the achievements of our communities' leaders. LGBTQ+ leaders are there to lead, first and foremost.

Our sexuality isn't the sole defining piece about who we are. When I came out, this was something I repeated to people over and over again "I have not changed, I am just happier. I am just me."

9

Leading through Truth, Trust, and Pixie Dust

If it's not clear to the world yet, words matter—no pressure for someone writing a book that is nothing but words. The words we choose to use and the words we are forced to hear have an incredible impact on the future of our society, especially when they come from leaders. Our community's history was often told through those who had the power of the pen. Now that power has shifted to the power of presence. Anyone, regardless of the size of their network or social media followers, has some presence and some power to shape the perspective of those in their circle, the power to share information, and the power to lead.

A leader isn't someone you just follow, it's someone who you trust and someone who is honest, even when they don't have all the answers. A queer leader is also someone who lives their truth and shares that with others regardless of how painful that may be. They are outspoken and unafraid to raise the concerns of their community. Through the act of coming out we, as a community, exercise our ability to live our truth. We learn how to be transparent and straightforward, and through this, we develop trust.

TRUTH, NO SHADE

Truth and transparency are two core values of mine, and I often lump them together to say I am an "honest" person. Not only do I believe you need to be both truthful and transparent to be an honest person, but I also assert that honesty is subjective to the person sharing the information. To me, it's the difference between being honest and saying, "I believe the sky is blue" versus being truthful when saying "the sky is blue." Being truthful is a matter of fact and emotions are removed from the equation, and ultimately, from the decision. When you lead through truth you are also able to have difficult and transparent conversations where the problem is addressed, and the team or organization isn't slowed down through emotionally charged conversations. Instead of leading with emotion, we lead with empathy, and instead of leading with beliefs, we lead with values and truths.

At the same time, it is important to keep in mind that leading through truth and transparency does not give you the license to be disrespectful. Truth does not mean disrespect; the world does not operate like an episode of RuPaul's Drag Race, and you're not going to build trust by being a shady queen. Remember that truth is supposed to be free from emotions and is a statement of facts. You may feel this way or that way about a certain colleague, and you may value direct and even brutal honesty, but where is that really going to get you? Leadership means pulling as much, if not more, weight for the team, not trying to lighten the load by cutting and betraying them.

Transparency operates similarly. Entering an organization or a role in the community with a hidden agenda is a sure way to hinder the development of trust between you and your colleagues, constituents, or community. If you're leading a team, regardless of the size, it can only help to be transparent with them. It provides clear guidance and understanding of the expectations at hand. Communication becomes horizontal instead of vertical when transparency is brought into the organization, especially those that have traditional hierarchies. Those from the LGBTQ+ and communities of color don't succeed at these organizations, or don't even get their foot through the door, because of the convoluted processes shrouded in mystery and reinforced through systems meant to keep marginalized communities out. Just look around. The Oscars, the Grammys, the Golden Globes, and the elected offices across our country, continue to look a certain way because the process is inherently opaque.

LGBTQ+ leaders must lead with transparency, truth, and trust. They are the core of resilience, and they are at the core of leadership. Realizing that life is complicated requires transparency, checking-in with yourself to have honest conversations requires truth and being able to focus on the positive rather than the negative, and being okay with gradual change requires trust in yourself and the process. Leaders must ask themselves if they are courageous enough to abandon the past and go forward into the unknown. A leap of faith doesn't require faith at all, but it requires you to be transparent about your goals, truthful about your intentions, and trusting that you are capable of taking yourself there and bring others with you.

FROM CHIEF EXECUTIVE TO COMMANDER-IN-CHIEF

Transparency, truth, and trust all sound like rules to live by or seem like they should be rules by which to run a campaign. A little-known mayor at the time made these part of his campaign platform for president of the United States and then wrote a book on the importance of trust in rebuilding America after four years of Trump in the White House. This mayor, turned Democratic candidate, turned cabinet secretary, is none-other than Pete Buttigieg. Secretary Buttigieg, still fondly referred to by many as Mayor Pete or just Pete as if we were all on a first name basis with him, was the first openly LGBTQ+ person confirmed by the United States Senate to serve as a cabinet secretary. He was confirmed by the US Senate in February 2021, by a vote of eighty-six in favor and thirteen opposed as secretary of transportation (AP, 2021). He was also the first openly gay Democratic presidential candidate during the 2020 elections.

Remember that fancy-sounding fundraising event for the Victory Fund, "the National Champagne Brunch," that I mentioned a while back before we went on a deep fan moment of Danica Roem? Well, it was at that event that I first saw Senator Pete. Back then, he was still only Mayor Pete, but we all knew he would soon announce his run for president of the United States. Now before you get excited, no I have not yet met Pete Buttigieg or his husband Chasten, but my husband did have his first "Buttigieg sighting" early into his term as secretary of transportation. Pete had already been on my radar for some time before he graced that ball-room full of eager gays at the brunch. There were rumors and speculations that this mayor from South Bend, Indiana, was going after the highest office in the land and everyone was trying to get their moment with the possible next president of the United States.

As I stood in the crowded doorframe of the ballroom at some hotel in Washington, DC, I heard Buttigieg speak for the first time. I don't know why I expected him to make the announcement "I am running for president" there and then without thinking that he would go on to do this in his hometown of South Bend. He could have talked about a multitude of things, he could have spoken about a potential policy platform, he could have spoken about how he was different from the already crowded list of Democratic hopefuls, or he could have spoken about how his sexuality was going to be an asset to the campaign. He was still in an "exploratory phase" for his run for president. Instead, he chose to open up about a personally difficult subject, one that many within the LGBTQ+ community face—shame.

"If you had offered me a pill to make me straight, I would have swallowed it before you had time to give me a sip of water. It is a hard thing to think about now. It's hard to face the truth that there were times in my life when if you had shown me exactly what it was inside me that made me gay, I would have cut it out with a knife. And the reason is so awful to think about isn't just the knowledge that so many young people struggling to come to terms with their sexuality or their gender identity, do just that, they harm themselves, figuratively or literally. But the real reason that it's so hard to think about is if I had

had the chance to do that, I would never have found my way to Chasten. That the best thing in my life. My marriage might not have happened at all.

My marriage. This thing I can't even describe without going into cliches like talking about how my world went from black and white to color the moment we held hands toward the end of our first day. The thing that made it possible for me to get through the loss of my father this year. This man who lifted up not just me, but dad and mom through those last awful days. How dark the thought that the man that I admire and care about and love sharing with the rest of the country and even more importantly, can't wait to share one day with raising children might not have been part of my life at all. Thank God, there was no pill. Thank God, there was no knife."

He was transparent, and he was truthful about the shame that many LGBTQ+ individuals feel at some point in their lives, if not throughout their entire lives. We are raised in a global society that makes us feel less than and that makes us feel as if we should hide who we are. It is unexplainable, the feeling that many of us within the LGBTQ+ community felt with having Pete get close to securing the nomination. Just think about it, a gay mayor from the middle of the country outlasted several prominent senators and representatives, and several millionaires and billionaires with the personal funds to keep their campaigns marching on.

Despite the pressure, the long hours, and his relatively new-found recognition, Mayor Pete Buttigieg required a very different set of experiences to not just succeed but shine through a crowded field of close to thirty Democratic presidential hopefuls. Through every debate, interview, loaded question, and long night on the campaign trail, Pete showed resilience. Regardless of your politics, you must recognize that it took an unmatched level of resilience to campaign and win the critical Iowa Caucus as the first, openly gay millennial.

By declaring "I'm running for president of the United States," Pete had pushed open the door for future generations of LGBTQ+ elected officials to look towards the highest office in the land with hope. You can bet that he won't be the last gay millennial to utter those words.

BEYOND THE BINARY

Letting people into your personal life takes a lot of courage, vulnerability, and a tremendous amount of resilience. When discussing his memoir *"Over the Top"* Jonathan Van Ness (JVN) shared in an interview with the Audible UK, "It's nerve-racking, I wonder if people would still love me as much as they knew like what my whole story was." Many of us go to meet JVN through the lens of Netflix's *Queer Eye* from where we all picked up the phrase, "Can you believe?" and added that into our daily vocabulary. Yes, because we share the same name, he is my favorite. Throughout the show, JVN was constantly an outspoken breath of fresh air in heavy moments and situations throughout the series. We all got to know him through this upbeat and bubbly persona on the show that made us binge-watch season after season.

By the time their memoir came out, we were already five seasons deep into *Queer Eye* and had become infatuated with the cast. JVN says that while he never really had to come out, he didn't realize there was another option for gender identification until later in life. JVN shared in a conversation about his memoir what it was like to discover the possibility beyond the binary. JVN identifies as nonbinary and uses he/they/she pronouns though prefers he/him (Tirado, 2019). In the same candid interview with Audible UK JVN shared,

"I had been saying 'oh I'm a cisgender gay man…' and at some point I that was like, 'I don't know. Prior to that, when I started going back and forth between New York and LA I got just much more immersed in like a gorgeous vibrant LGBTQ community that exists in New York that I didn't really have the same sort of access to in Los Angeles. And that's when I started realizing, okay there is more than a binary for me to, subscribe, or in this case unsubscribe from…I never really identified as a man, I think I just thought that that was my only choice."

JVN wants us to destigmatize shame and understand that it is normal. Normalizing shame wasn't easy for JVN, but he describes it as incredibly liberating. This embodies the ability for LGBTQ+ leaders to be truthful, transparent, and develop trust with a broader community.

Part of what makes JVN an incredibly resilient leader within our community is his perspective on history and his understanding that our community was so deeply impacted and almost erased by the lack of support during the start of the AIDS pandemic in the early 1980s. While speaking about his memoir, JVN shares this understanding of privilege and perspective as it relates to our own LGBTQ+ history.

"No, I mean I can really live all the way authentically and my truth is someone who is living with HIV and someone who is a survivor of abuse and someone who is engaged in recovery from compulsivity and like a whole deluge of areas. So it's nice just to be able to be open and authentic about the path that I've taken to be here. And then I definitely am the person that you know and love from Queer Eye but I'm also someone who has other things going on that are really important to talk about.

Giving justice to the people and giving voice to people that are living with HIV giving voice to people that don't get to be here any longer because of HIV and all the inadequacies and racism and homophobia that caused us to lose a whole generation of people in facilities for personally affecting people of color and marginalized communities I think sometimes that I shouldn't be having like so much fun all the time like they need to be talking about these other aspects that affect my life like very deeply that you wouldn't really see on Queer Eye but I needed to be able to talk about all those things together."

Shame within the LGBTQ+ community, better known as internalized homophobia, makes us question how we dress, how we present ourselves for a job interview, and even what we tap the like button for on social media. Transparently living our truth, we shouldn't have to justify why we chose to wear that skirt to a job interview, why we don't do this or do that. Our bodies, our actions, and our thoughts aren't meant to be policed by those outside of, or even within, our community. As a cisgender gay man, I am immensely privileged to go throughout life benefiting from many of the social systems set in place. The same does not hold true for members of the trans community.

A FANTASTIC WOMAN

Actor Daniela Vega may not be a common household name in the United States, but she is a powerhouse artist and activist in Chile. For many Latin Americans, Chile for so long presented a model of an advanced economy and stable nation in the region. Despite being a point of pride of Chile after *A Fantastic Woman* won the Oscar for Best Foreign Language Film at the ninetieth Academy Awards in 2018, Vega returned to Chile where her name and gender were not legally recognized. Until December 2019, Chile did not have any sort of legal protection for gender identity. This forced Daniela Vega, a trans woman, to go through the stressful, and often triggering process of needing to utilize her deadname, or her former birth name, when interacting with formal institutions of the government, such as customs.

Chile had previously won one other Academy Award, in the Best Animated Short Film category at the eighty-eighth Academy Awards in 2016 for *Bear Story*. Ironically, or maybe very much appropriately, both of these films highlighted aspects of Chile that broke the perceptions of the country. *Bear Story* focused on life in Chile's past under the dictatorship of Pinochet and *A Fantastic Woman* focused on the very contemporary struggles of being trans in a society set up to make you feel invisible. Daniela Vega boldly called out the Chilean government at a press conference upon returning to Chile after winning the Oscar.

"In this country that I am returning to along with my happy team, on my ID there is a name that is not my name because the country where I was born does not grant me that possibility. Time passes, the clock continues to run, and people

leave hoping that one day this will be changed. And today a movie appears that does not pretend to be the guiding light but instead asks where is what we have been looking for. This, at least for me, is the significance of having done this with this team of men and women who were willing to put human emotions at the service of other human beings and to ask themselves why not instead of how come" (Leon, 2018).

We can't place the burden of trans rights being human rights on Chile if we here in the United States still have so much progress to make. After all, Daniela Vega was the first trans actor to present an award at the ninetieth Oscars. According to the Human Rights Campaign, 2020 was the deadliest year on record for members of the trans community and these are only the deaths that we know of, the deaths that made headlines or were brought to the attention of the masses (HRC, 2020). How many trans members, how many gender non-conforming individuals, have we lost to the silence of shame in the United States alone?

Leading through transparency and leading with truth in all that we do shouldn't just apply to the LGBTQ+ community, but should be used by all leaders around the globe. The communities which we serve through our art, policies, and spaces we take up in the community deserve to be led in this way. Our community, the LGBTQ+ community, deserves the freedom to be transparent and true to our community and ourselves. Life may be complicated, and resilient leaders know that, but through transparency and truth, we can build trust. Trust in ourselves and our abilities, trust that we are meant to lead in each and every space that we reside within, and trust that those who still need us will march right through the door and demand our seat at the table. We have chairs. Trust me, we are also willing to stand as long as we need to and demand representation, inclusion, and equality.

10

Leading through Empathy

———

Lesbian, Gay, Bisexual, Transgender, Queer, Intersex, Two-Spirit—what comes to mind? Who comes to mind? How would you describe them? Now, if your first thought about any of these sexualities or gender identities is something negative, if you thought that one doesn't or shouldn't exist, or if your body recoiled, your heart is pumping with anxiety, and you currently are sitting in something closer to a fetal position rather a comfortable way to read a book, I need you to stop and think. Our community is way more than the cisgender white gay men that the media has recently begun to typecast as representative of our community... I'm looking at you, Hallmark.

Before I continue, it's important for me to recognize the immense privilege that I possess. Simply by appearance, I am a white cisgender gay man able to pass through this world without the immediate barriers faced by other members of the community, especially the trans members of our community and especially those of color. I recognize that depending on the day, and honestly, what I'm wearing that day, you're unlikely to look at me and go "'gasp!' he is gay!" I thought for a while that this was a good thing, that I could go unperceived through a space, especially a professional setting, without giving any sort of indication to my sexuality. I recognize that this is based on heteronormative standards that have dominated my upbringing, but that also continues to dominate many professional spaces today. Only respecting queer people who pass as straight, by societal standards, is not respecting queer people and this is not negotiable.

This is changing, we are truly the queer generation, and these standards and norms are making way to more open and diverse spaces.

CONFIDENCE IS SEXY

Our communities share a story of resilience in the face of constant adversity throughout our lives. Those most critical moments help develop leadership capabilities within us at a much younger age. One of these is the ability to express empathy to a wider community, but with a keen eye towards those who have faced discrimination and adversity. Champions in this area can harness their stories: their coming out stories, their stories of facing bullying in too many spaces, their stories of perseverance and triumph, to show, even as cliché as it may sound, that it truly does get better.

Spending twenty-one years in the closet will place certain mental and physical roadblocks along your way, but by even attempting to unlearn them I have been able to excel in both my professional and personal life. I applaud any individual, regardless of their gender or sexual orientation, who is willing to strap on a pair of heels and walk out of their door. That takes an immense amount of courage and confidence, even more so if you're about "to put on the wigs and the heels, and the lashes and the hair, and take the train to the club" (Scissor Sisters, 2011). If you don't know this reference, please look it up so you're prepared for your next kiki.

Though it is unlikely you'll ever catch me walking into a room with heels on—my Chelsea boots with a significant heel don't count regardless of how much sparkle they may have—I have learned, however, to confidently walk into a room with a bag, or a purse, or a man bag, whatever you want to call them. They are by far more comfortable than a backpack, which just ends up digging at your shoulders and won't make me look and reemphasize the intern vibe that I apparently give off – good skincare y'all. Thank you, Juan.

A TECHNICAL SKILL
Unlike other communities and identity groups, the LGBTQ+ community isn't brought together because of common ancestry or a common language. Okay well some might argue though that the zoological categorization of gay men may seem like its own language or phrases like "spilling/sipping tea" and "reading" have vastly different meanings, depending on the community. We exist on every continent and in every country, region, and city of the world. We speak the world's languages, share in the world's multiple belief systems and faiths, and have vastly different political ideologies; in the

United States, some are even, dare I say, Republicans and voted for Trump in the 2016 and 2020 elections.

When you really take the time to think about it, we don't share that much in common. We are a group of individuals that are lumped together because we either don't like the gender we are supposed to like, or our gender identity and gender markers don't align with who we are. Even with this slight common thread among us all, we still don't like the same gender or don't agree which aspects of one's identities constitute being of one gender versus another. What is gender, anyway, other than a social construct that has traditionally kept one gender, female, as secondary to the male gender? When you zoom out and look at the broad and diverse LGBTQ+ community, it does sound like what we have in common is an issue with the entire artificial concept of gender.

However, there is more to it. Our community is connected by the lived experiences we all share. The common thread of struggle and adversity often transforms into resilience. The community faces increased discrimination in their personal lives, the workplace, the public space, and when accessing critical resources. According to the Center for American Progress, more than one in three members of the community faced discrimination of some kind in a year. This number increases to a staggering three out of five transgender Americans, and over 50 percent report hiding a personal relationship or altering aspects of their personal or work life in order to avoid discrimination.

LGBTQ+ Americans even go as far as postponing or avoiding medical treatment to avoid instances of discrimination.

Members of the LGBTQ+ community are three times as likely to experience mental health disorders, with substance abuse issues and mental illnesses reportedly double that of their straight counterparts. Even though LGBTQ+ youth is estimated to be 7 percent of the general youth population, they make up 40 percent of the homeless youth population. The main reason for being homeless? They were forced out of their homes for simply being themselves.

There are leaders who can lead through empathy. It is "an action of understanding, being aware of, being sensitive to, and vicariously experiencing the feelings, thoughts, and experiences of another, of either the past or present without having the feelings, thoughts, and experience fully communicated in an objectively explicit manner" according to our good friends over at Merriam-Webster. Essentially, empathetic leaders can lead by and with an understanding of others, their stories, and experiences without ever necessarily having experienced them firsthand.

People are told to lead with empathy as if it just requires you to be nicer to others or to listen more closely when engaging in a conversation. Sure, these are part of it, but empathy is a skill that needs to be exercised and curated over time; it is not just something that can be mastered overnight. Just like resilience, empathy is a realization that life is complicated and that we need to focus on the positive rather than the negative. More importantly, empathetic leadership, just like resilient leadership, requires the ability to check-in with oneself and have an honest conversation. It is a gradual skill that takes a holistic approach to understand an individual or a situation.

More so, empathy isn't some sort of frivolous soft skill meant to be undervalued in comparison to some sort of hard technical skill. What makes Apple's Genius bar so incredible? Sure, they can solve my very technical complicated problem, even if that issue was only technically complicated to me, but it's more impressive that they do it with grace and a certain understanding that we are all different. Even the United States Army repeatedly mentions empathy as a critical skill needed to be an effective leader as part of their Leader Development Field Manual.

To the Army "leaders of character adhere to the Army values, display empathy, and the Warrior Ethos/Service Ethos, and practice good discipline." The field manual goes into this further and describes the competency development of empathy into three categories where the standard competency for empathy is described as "demonstrate[ing] an understanding of another person's point of view. Identifies with others' feelings and emotions. Displays a desire to care for Soldiers, Army Civilians, and others" (Army, 2015).

Displaying a strength, or mastery, of empathy means to be "attentive to other's views and concerns. It takes personal action to improve the situation of soldiers, army, civilians, family members, local community, and even that of potential adversaries. Breaks into training, coaching, or counseling mode when needed and role models empathy for others" (Army, 2015). If you were to take out the words "soldiers," "army," and "civilians" from that description of having a strength in empathy, it is easy to see how the LGBTQ+ community embodies a strength of empathy. We take personal action to improve the lives of those around us, we make our communities better. We try, keyword: *try*, to educate and guide those who may be against us.

In our defense, there is no mention of having to be patient or wait around for "adversaries" to come to their senses. So don't boo, vote. Don't get mad, get elected.

Empathy isn't the same as simply being nice or making people happy. It is the ability to listen closely, analyze a situation critically, see others (even if it is the opposition's point of view), and be able to then respond. Even with all of this, you could still respond by saying something like "I understand your point of view and can see how this would be an exciting project for our organization to take on, but at this moment we don't have the financial liberty to adequately carry out that program. Could you put a proposal together however, to have ready for when funds free up and we can circle back to this initiative?" In this case, the hypothetical employee is actively listened to, a fact-based assertion and response were given, and in this particular case, the suggestion was not flat out rejected but placed on hold when both parties can come back to the table with more information, resources, and time.

Empathy, when combined with resilience, is an undeniable powerhouse skill set to possess regardless of industry. Add a foundation and set of values based on the queer perspective and you have the potential for great leadership. These are individuals who have faced adversity in their own life, often throughout their entire life, yet somehow keep smiling, are optimistic, and bounce right back. It seems as if they don't have bad days, just bad moments.

REPRESENTATION MATTERS

I'm a very proud Hoya for many reasons, not just because I need to be proud since I will be paying back my student loans for decades. What is a Hoya? Yes. Georgetown may not teach empathy, but spending four years on the Hilltop makes one aware of its power and influence. Georgetown produces some incredible alumni who embody the value of being "people for others" and going out into the world to genuinely try to enact positive change.

One of these individuals is none other than Reggie Greer, a graduate of the College class of 2009 with a degree in Government and History. In the world of LGBTQ+ politics, especially in Washington, DC, you say the name Reggie and people can't help but smile and be positive. I had the incredible opportunity to work with Greer when he was director of constituent engagement at the Victory Institute where I was a graduate intern with the leadership team. Reggie knows everyone in Washington and probably every LGBTQ+ elected official in the country. When I say that Greer knows everyone, I mean it in a genuine manner. He listens to people, hears them, and pays attention to every word, every concern, every hope and dream that they have. Reggie asking, "How are you?" is with actual interest in your life, not just with the expectation that you would say, "doing well" and move on.

This is likely why President Biden named Greer LGBTQ+ liaison for the Biden campaign in March during the primaries. After President Biden became the presumptive Democratic nominee, Reggie Greer then became the director for LGBTQ+ Voter Outreach for the remainder of the campaign. He was then brought on early into the transition and finally into the Biden-Harris White House as director of priority placement, and senior LGBTQ+ advisor. It also helps that he was no stranger to building support for a cause, since he was previously appointed by President Obama as deputy director for Public Engagement at the US Department of Transportation. Now even though transportation impacts the day-to-day lives of every American, it is unlikely to be at the forefront of Americans' minds when they think of the president's cabinet. So, if anyone could get the public to engage with the DOT it was Reggie Greer.

Greer is no stranger to adversity and the intersectionality of identities and this likely made him an incredible advocate and spokesperson for the Biden campaign and administration. He is a Texan, a Black man, a gay man, and a disabled man. He describes in his piece in *Out Magazine* that,

"Growing up and dealing with the complications of hemifacial microsomia, a degenerative birth defect that affects one out of every ten-thousand births, was not easy, but I learned early on to make this journey my own. I had just completed my nineteenth surgery, three months removed from my seventeenth birthday. While most rising high school seniors were working summer jobs, hanging out with friends, or planning for their last year in school before college, I found myself in my personal purgatory — a place not good, but also not bad. Years later, when I came out as gay to my parents, I remembered how impactful it had been for me to lean into my truth and embrace all of the qualities that make up who I am. My parents, born into religious households in the segregated South, reciprocated with even more love and acceptance, thus reinforcing everything I had come to believe" (Greer, 2015).

Yes, the LGBTQ+ community faces its own unique set of challenges and setbacks, but let's call them opportunities. We are presented with opportunities much younger in life than our straight cisgender counterparts to explore our leadership qualities and potential. Much earlier than one should, or than one would expect, we are denied the opportunities to win a participation trophy and we are only given wins or losses. We either won because we survived another homophobic remark or action or because we were allowed to go about our day without the need to defend or explain our existence.

Many of us go through our lives having to allocate our time to defend our queer identity while also standing up for the multiple intersections of identity we inhabit ranging from race and ability to socioeconomic and even political ideology. As Reggie Greer so rightly puts it, "the LGBTQ + community is extremely diverse, spanning the complete spectrum of America's social, racial, and cultural landscape" (OUT, 2020). There is simultaneously almost nothing that truly binds the wide and diverse LGBTQ+ community like our collective lived experience. We understand what it means to struggle, persevere, and bring a sense of resilience into every room in which we take up space. We understand what it's like not just to walk a mile in someone else's Dr. Martens but to also empathize with the literal weight of putting one foot in front of the other.

11

Leading Unapologetically

—

Queer kids are just like their hetero counterparts: susceptible and easy to mold at a young age. Impressionable to a fault, they take social cues from their fellow peers, adults in their lives, and their community. While all of this has an immense impact on the development of any child, this impact is magnified in LGBTQ+ youth given the limited ability to see themselves in other children, the adults around them, both at home and in formal settings like schools, and in the wider community. Straight kids, on the other hand, never have to come out or explain when they knew they were attracted to the opposite sex. From day one, whether they know it or not, queer kids are forced to fend for themselves and find clever ways to adapt to the world around them. We find our voice, our authenticity, and our ability to be unapologetically ourselves.

MEJOR TARDE, QUE CON SUEÑO

Back home from college freshman year, I found myself alone with my mom on a weekday. We were spending the afternoon at some outlet mall or shopping center outside of Austin. I had introduced my mom to Pad Thai from P.F. Chang's, which had just been introduced to me in DC. She didn't like it. Regardless of the discovery of her dislike for one of the most quintessential Thai dishes, that was the first time my mom straight up asked me, "Are you gay?" Maybe there is some unknown connection between Asian noodles and moms asking their sons if they are gay, but I'll leave that to some grad students looking for an interesting thesis idea.

The shocked look on my face must have been priceless, my reaction very similar to the meme of Miss Jay Alexander from America's Next Top Model reaching for his neck, which looking back, was probably a very clear indication that I was, in fact, gay. However, I—in typical closeted fashion—had already come up with a response for every possible question that could ever be thrown at me trying to pry open the closet door, especially one as direct as "Are you gay?" My response, at least in my head, was a calm, cool and collected, yet firm, "No," followed immediately by "What would give you that idea?" in the hopes of figuring out what signal I had unintentionally given off that had led to this conclusion. My mom responded, in typical mom fashion, "There is nothing wrong with being gay." I thought to myself, *then why ask*? Likely, because all moms have some sort of mind-reading capability, she filled the silence with the answer to my question. "It's just because you're always defending LGBTQ+ people. Whenever someone says something negative about them, you're the first to stand up for them."

This was true then and is even more true now. I felt the urge to stand up for a community to which I was not ready to admit I belonged, but knew on some deep level that I needed to defend. My response was probably something along the lines of, "I have friends that are gay, we have family members, though distant, that are out, and someone has to stand up for them. It's important to stand up for communities that are being hurt, discriminated against, and otherwise marginalized by institutions and systems of which we are all a part." I probably received some sort of confused look that questioned why I was so passionate about defending a community I wasn't a part of... yet.

At the time, I was enrolled in the Georgetown University School of Foreign Service with the naive dream of eventually joining the US Foreign Service and working in the Middle East, specifically Saudi Arabia, the United Arab Emirates, Kuwait, and Qatar. My passion for defending and standing up for human rights led me to focus my studies on the Arab Gulf, not because I had some inflated white savior complex, but because I knew and saw just how much fear people had of the region, especially countries with such contrasting government and cultural norms. After all, my generation is the product of a post-September 11 world.

At seven years old, the events of September 11 should not be vividly engraved in my mind, yet I remember the teacher rolling in the boxy black-and-brown TV on one of those four-foot-tall black metal shelf contraptions. She proceeded to turn on the news, and a room full of second graders watched as the second plane crashed into the World Trade Center on the morning of September 11, 2001. I, being confused, asking myself why we as children were watching these events happen live. As a nation, we were forever marked and changed on that day.

Even as a kid, I could see just how quickly fear took over our collective decision-making. The United States continues to have a problem with racism and discrimination. Full stop non-negotiable. My entire life before coming out was shaped by this attack and by the fear that took over the nation. While this moment may have shaped me and would eventually lead me to my degree in international affairs, it probably also delayed my coming out by several years. Anything that was different, especially in Texas, was quickly signaled as a threat.

I remember being policed by that very same second-grade teacher, who permanently engraved September 11 into my consciousness, for speaking Spanish in the classroom. At home, we spoke only Spanish, and I was still part of the English as a Second Language (ESL) program at an elementary school that was predominantly filled with Latino students. Spanish was the language I felt most comfortable speaking, especially with friends. It's the language I still feel most comfortable in expressing certain emotions and feelings. To me, speaking Spanish isn't something weird. It most surely isn't a threat. I guess the thought of a Spanish speaker being able to go forth and master two languages simultaneously may have been intimidating. After all, if Mexicans were apparently already stealing jobs, imagine what an educated and bilingual Mexican could do!

At this young age, I was already seeing how mean people could be. By the second grade, I had begun to understand that I wasn't like the other boys in my class, and this wasn't just because I spoke Spanish. This hate and xenophobia developing in the US awoke something unconscious in me that must have seen the danger in being different. This was a flag to me that it wasn't the right time to come out. So, before I could even develop an understanding of who I truly was, I let it slip away into some dark corner of my mind—into some closet—and hid the key.

Despite having the privilege of being white-passing, both because of the color of my skin and Irish last name, my mouth seemed to betray me early on in life. My fight, my day-to-day struggle, was to blend in as a Spanish speaker. I was unable to hide this as my tongue tripped over itself, and still does, over words like scissors, wolf, and the number forty. I was teased for speaking another language and often told by teachers that we spoke English in America. As much as I unwillingly tried to hide the way I rolled my 'r,' or the way I flowed in and out of both languages, I couldn't. Looking back, I shouldn't have dealt with this. Instead, my sexuality had to be hidden, so I focused on school and with each xenophobic attack, my queerness took a back seat to the challenge of my time.

In many ways, I am now making up for lost time: for the years that I couldn't stand up for my LGBTQ+ community and for being unable to live and lead unapologetically, but I'm here now. Like we say in Spanish "*mejor tarde, que con sueño*" or "better late than sleepy."

When we learn how to lead unapologetically depends on our surroundings and environment, but we get there.

Unapologetic leadership means you bring all of you to spaces you inhabit regardless of what others might think. Despite how controversial this type of leadership may be, it is necessary and interconnects with various aspects of queer, resilient leadership. Not only will unapologetic leaders know that life is complicated, but they will point it out and they will call out the systems set in place that make life more complicated for some more than others. They know how to have honest conversations with themselves but will also have very honest and very direct conversations with others. They focus and thrive in the positive, regardless of how small.

Leading unapologetically is the ability to lead and bring others with you.

LIVE, WORK, POSE!

If you want to talk about unapologetic leaders, then you don't have to go further than the three leading actors in *Pose* –MJ Rodriguez, Dominique Jackson, and Indya Moore.

I could go on and on about *Pose,* I could probably write an entire book about the impact that this show has had on not just my life, but the wider LGBTQ+ community, and what it has done for the representation of the transgender community. Luckily, there are three incredible seasons for you to binge, so I don't have to do the work because Ryan Murphy has done that already. Frankly, *Pose* has given our community a chance to see stories of our community told by and for us.

MJ RODRIGUEZ

As MJ Rodriguez, who portrays Blanca Rodriguez Evange-lista, a housemother on the show, puts it, "It's amazing to be able to speak for your community in a way, and it's also great to speak for a specific part of the community that has been ostracized for a long time, even though the LGBT community has been out there when it comes to pride and everything. Sometimes I feel like some of them get lost in the, in the mix and the 'T' was one of them they get lost in the mix" (Mondy, 2018). When the transgender community is portrayed in film, it's often as a reduction, not just to a stereotype of the queer community, but an ostracization and othering of a foun-dational part of our community. There would be no pride without trans women of color,

MJ goes on to share, "A lot of people forgot that African American women, Latino women, and women of color, who are of the trans experience, they forget that we were the women who kind of cultivated the ballroom culture in order for a lot of drag queens to be drag queens and a lot of gay men to live out their fantasy as far as being feminine and being comfortable in it. It's shows like this that give you a glimpse into the founding mothers, and how the founding fathers came along and how they created these children in order for us to be here today" (Mondy, 2018).

Pose shares stories about our community from our per-spective, and it showed the diversity of our community. No character falls within the trap of being perceived from the perspective of a cisgender, white, heterosexual society. Instead, there is a diversity of representation from within the community, a diversity of stories all having nothing to do with the sexual orientation or gender identity of the character and everything to do with the time and place they were living in. The show revolves around the very true and raw stories from our community during the 1980s and 1990s in New York City's ballroom culture. It dives deep into the perspectives of trans women, as told by trans women, and people of color during this time: stories that even the rest of the community fails, time and time again, to highlight.

DOMINIQUE JACKSON

Dominique Jackson, who plays Mother Elektra Wintour, is a staunch advocate, not just for the community as a whole, but especially for trans women of color. Nothing proves this point more than her incredible speech at the Human Rights Campaign's twenty-third annual dinner.

"We talk about love, but we forget about humanity. I am a human being. I am a human being just like each and every one of you. It is time that we stop with the aesthetic. It's time that we stop with the privilege. It is time that we realize that if one man has a billion dollars, and an entire community can benefit, if you just give of that billion dollars a million and help that community survive thing, then you're really doing something. You're a part of a community.

I say to each and every one of you tonight, and I'm not going to take up your time. But each and every one of you who has the ability to stand in this room has some kind of privilege. You have some kind of existence that you know. I am a woman that was ostracized. I'm a woman of Caribbean descent. I'm *a woman of transgender experience. I'm a woman. But some of you don't see that.*

We talk about Humanity we must see the human factor. Our foundation is human, not sex. It is not about us, saying to someone else that 'I accept you or I tolerate you'. You do not have the power to accept or tolerate me, I take that from you. You will respect me. So to each of you, my community dies every day whether it's from HIV and AIDS, or from transphobia, or homophobia I asked you, consider this, that is a human being. We are all human beings. It's about inclusivity and I will never, ever ask any of you for respect, I will demand it.

You will not tell me that you accept me, you will not tell me that you tolerate me. That is not your power. I take that from you. You will respect me for who I am. And I asked you, don't tolerate us, don't think that you have approval in our lives. Respect us for who we are."

Respect us for who we are not because we are asking for respect, but because we are demanding it. More and more LGBTQ+ leaders across our community are demanding respect and a seat at the table. We want to be more than just your spokesperson on LGBTQ+ issues during pride. We are not looking to help check off some diversity markers on your board of directors. We are knowledgeable about national security issues, the environment, and small business development. We are talented artists and actors, and we are incredible athletes across all sports. There may have been a time when asking us to serve on your board would have been good enough, but we are long past that time, and the new generation, one of the queerest in the history of our planet, demands a seat because we are just as uniquely qualified as other individuals who are there.

INDYA MOORE

Then, there is Indya Moore. They play Angel Evangelista on *Pose*. Not only are they a powerhouse actor, but an unstoppable and unapologetic fighting voice for the entire community. Indya was also the first-ever Black trans model to be on the cover of *Elle* magazine in 2019, giving them an opportunity to share their story with an audience that isn't used to hearing from Black trans women.

In the interview, Indya explains, "I don't know how to have fun," due to the constant fight to survive, which for them started at age fourteen when they entered the foster care system. "Because I was assigned male at birth, [my parents] expected me to be masculine or to perform the way they thought young boys should perform. And I did not. They didn't understand. They had never experienced what it was like to have a family member who was genderqueer" (Yuan, 2019).

Mundane conversations, such as what is Indya's favorite restaurant, seem difficult in a world where so much else is happening. "When I'm around people having conversations about their day, I'm looking at them, like, 'What could they possibly be talking about? How are we not talking about deconstructing white supremacy right now? How are we not trying to save trans people?' I don't know who I am outside of someone who's just trying to be free and find safety for myself and for others" (Yuan, 2019). In countless interviews,

Indya calls out the increasing injustices faced at large, and not just in the United States, but on a global stage too. They have used their meteoric rise to fame to cast a bright and direct light on these issues to their over a million, and growing, followers on Instagram alone. They have transparent and truthful conversations with thousands on topics that they are uniquely qualified to speak on because, well, they make up their lived experiences.

In an interview with *Dazed,* Indya shares, "I'm still working on myself and trying to use my platform to be of service to my people. I'm just a flawed human being with experiences and opinions, and I need to be able to be these things if I'm ever gonna not be at some point. It's a privilege to be able to be your best self constantly. Not everybody has the kind of history—the confidence and the support —that makes it easier to do that."

Pose has done so much for the community in terms of representation, but these actors have gone above and beyond to continue to use their platforms for good, to live and lead unapologetically. Indya has said that they don't look up or down at anyone and wishes that we looked "at" each other more. From first-hand experience, I can tell you that they do that. They look at you and are there with you

IT'S A SMALL WORLD

My husband, Juan, and I had found ourselves at *"the happiest place on earth"* in October of 2018, Disney World. Why were we there in the middle of the semester, I have no clue. The flights may have been cheap and well, we thought "why not?"

We had spent all day at Magic Kingdom and when I say all day, I truly mean all day. We had seen the fireworks show at this point. Me, being the way I am, said, "Well, if the parks are still open, I'm getting on something because I paid for these tickets already" and Disney isn't cheap. So, at this point, I'm like, "Why not get on Space Mountain?" A roller coaster. I'm terrified of heights and hate roller coasters, but I needed to get every dollar out of this trip.

Naturally, during the fireworks display, I was on Instagram. If you don't post a story that you're watching the fireworks, are you really even there? Since Instagram is a dangerously distracting app for me, I naturally began to be sucked in by other posts and stories casually without giving it much thought. Then I lost it. I let out a little yelp, the type of yelp that annoys my husband because it means I'm about to be annoying or give an unsolicited Ted Talk.

They were there! It was either Indya's or MJ's story, but suddenly I noticed that they were at Disney. Immediately I thought, "Oh, this must be a late post" because *Pose* had just aired their first season only months before, and there was no way these celebs would be posting their location in real time. I shoved the bright screen at my husband screaming, "Look who is here!" He then calmly responded; no, they are here. He must have put two and two together, maybe some story of the fireworks showed that closely matched what we had just seen.

As we made our way to Space Mountain, I saw people running through the lines, hopping the chains, quickly making their way to the front. I noticed that it was none other than

Mother Elektra, then I noticed Angel, and finally, Blanca. I must have yanked my husband because he isn't one to move fast, much more of a leisurely stroller, and I dragged him through the chains, making our way closer and closer to them. Now you would think that having met politicians would have prepared me to be calm, cool, and collected when I met them. I wasn't.

Indya Moore was getting on the ride when the Disney employee told them they couldn't get on the ride with their empty Mickey Mouse cup. The staff, very respectfully I'm sure, said they had to drop it off with them and could pick it up after. After all, you are getting on a roller coaster, right? To this day I have no idea what took over me to scream from several rows back "I will hold their cup!"

As the staff looked at me with a confused, yet very warranted look, they took Indya's cup and placed it where they would be getting off the ride and pressed "go." I couldn't have cared less about getting my money's worth for that ride. I don't even know if I screamed while on the ride, I don't even remember the ride, to be honest, I just remember wanting to get off. When the less-than-thirty-second ride was over, I did what any self-respecting fan would do; I tried to find Moore. I have never in my life chased after a celeb or politician. I don't even run to cross crosswalks, but wow did I run to find them. It was more of a fast waddle if we're being honest though, because the hubby wasn't moving too fast.

Luckily, the cast was trying to get on the ride again and, as they crisscrossed the ropes, I went up to the side and awkwardly got their attention. Immediately I apologized for interrupting their vacation and thanked them for being a voice for our wider community and told them how incredible they were on *Pose*. I was stunned by their generosity with their time, how incredibly nice and honest they were, and yes, Dominique's height. They seemed stunned that someone recognized them after just one season and genuinely grateful that their show was having an impact. All three of them smiled, took the time to give Juan and me hugs, take pictures, and have a genuine conversation.

Obviously, that picture went up on social media and yes, they did like the photo if you're wondering. To this day, I don't know if Indya Moore ever got their cup back, but I do know that it truly is a "small world after all."

Queer people need to take up space at the table and make space for other members of our community. We need to be ready to lead and do so unapologetically. If there isn't a free seat at the table then we shouldn't have to bring our own. Instead, we should find a new table.

12

Leading through Community

———

You do know that every queer person leaves behind a trail of glitter and the smell of fresh flowers and expensive beauty products in the air, right? A unicorn gets a horn when a queer baby is born, but we can only see them... that's also why we are obsessed with them. At some point, we finally realize that we can see these unicorns and it clicks that we are, dare I say, unique.

Yeah, it's nothing like that. Don't worry, you're not missing out on unicorns.

Though it may be true that you can't pick the family that you're born into, you can certainly pick the family you keep. Family in our community takes on an entirely new meaning. There is, and will always be, the biological family that you're born into. We don't have much of a say in who is part of that group, and though we may grow distant from members, unfortunately, some are still related to us. Then, there is our chosen family. As the name suggest, this is the family we choose to have. Sure, some may be members of our biological family, but this extends to friends, mentors, and those in our lives who are part of our authentic existence.

Community is an important part of the wider queer culture. When we really look at it, there may not be many things other than the shared experiences facing adversity that brings us together. Yet, we have community. Leading through community in queer spaces, and truly leading in the LGBTQ+ context, means being able to include all the diverse aspects of our community in the decision-making progress. Unlike traditional forms of leadership that may focus on influence or capabilities of one individual at the top because of their philosophy, policy, or charisma, queer community leadership requires the ability to do that while also uplifting thousands with you. Leadership in the LGBTQ+ community should mean recognizing the generations who struggled and fought for our rights to get us to this point. It should mean recognizing the individuals who not only opened the door but made sure that door stayed open for the next generation to walk through it.

The success of the next generation of queer leaders will depend on their ability to remember where we came from. Community is the essential lifeline for our fight for equality. Community is pride and we must also have pride in community.

WE ARE FAMILY...
Community is a word we likely have become accustomed to throwing around without a clear understanding of what

it means. Academically, according to Merriam-Webster, it means, "a unified body of individuals: such as the people with common interest living in a particular area." This could apply to some subset of the LGBTQ+ community, but it is unlikely to be able to encompass all of us given that we aren't living in a particular area. Let us try another definition by the all-knowing Webster, "a group of people with a common characteristic, living together within a larger society, or even a body of persons or nations having a common history or common social, economic, and political interests." This broader definition is helpful, but just like other communities, we may not all have a common social, economic, and political interest. While in the United States we fought for marriage equality, there are still countries around the world where our queer community is fighting for visibility and the right to exist.

How do we define queer community then? That's the beauty and the difficulty with our community. The inability to define us has been tremendously helpful in situations of danger, such as during Hitler's Germany. The lack of definition of "gay" made it virtually impossible to pinpoint exactly who belonged to our community. At the same time, the lack of collective cohesion makes the argument that we don't need unique rights an easy one for the opposition because there will be queers on both sides of the argument.

Specifically, within the United States, we have seen just how divisive the 2016 and 2020 presidential elections were. Just when we thought that the highest of glass ceilings would be shattered with the election of Hillary Clinton as the first female president of the United States, many of us saw our hopes and dreams shattered instead. We can't deny, however, that there was a group within the queer community that voted for Trump. In 2016, he received fourteen percent of the LGBTQ+ vote, which was doubled in 2020 when he secured twenty-eight percent (Broverman, 2016), despite his continued attack on members of the transgender community.

...WELL, SORT OF

Taking a step back, I don't even think that individuals who self-identify as LGBTQ+ have a good understanding of what community means. In an almost hour-long video by *Vice* media, published in 2019, a group of individuals, who all identified as belonging to the LGBTQ+ community, discussed political ideology and social issues (VICE, 2019). Even among this group of a dozen or so individuals from all identities and across the political spectrum, no consensus could be built on a single issue. Sarah Longwell, who participated in this discussion on Vice, identifies as a Republican and a lesbian. She is the president and CEO of Longwell Partners, an organization dedicated to building "uncommon coalitions that work together in common purpose" (Longwell, 2021).

Sarah highlights one of the issues at the core of our sense of community.

"I can't believe that you got twelve gay people here and no one feels at home in the gay community. Look, each of us has our own individual experiences, right? We're all humans who just want to like live in the world and be accepted for who we are. That was sort of what the community used to be. I think part of what we're suffering from is the difference between what

we meant to be a community of people that was all across the spectrum, to being shoehorned into a political movement. You know, the idea that we all have to row in the same direction politically, is, I think, a problem for us as a community" (VICE, 2019).

Our community is incredibly diverse beyond the singular stereotypes that have dominated the media. Our community may be predominantly liberal, but the politicization of our community won't always favor just one party or one elected official. The ability to lead within our community requires that leaders realize that there is no black and white to our community. We aren't like a coin you can flip with a guarantee of one of two options.

QUEERING RELIGION
Faith is something in which many think the LGBTQ+ community does not participate as well. After all, some of the biggest criticisms and sources of suffering for our community have come from the institutions of organized religion. Just think about the phrase "pray the gay away." Fortunately, I have encountered very few instances of overt homophobia. One of the most damaging, however, came from someone rather close to me who used religion as an excuse for their homophobia. They simply weren't afraid to hide it, were direct, and were disappointed in my "life choices" that conflicted directly with their beliefs of how I was choosing to live in sin. They told me they would "pray" for my salvation. Needless to say, because of their choices, our lives quickly took separate paths.

Books and movies such as *"Boy Erased: A Memoir"* by Garrard Conley and Hasan Namir's *God in Pink,* bring up necessary conversations about how faith is still used to demonize the LGBTQ+ community. Garrard's memoir focuses on the terrible practice of conversion therapy taking place, to this day, in Arkansas under the premise that it "cures" homosexuality. There is no cure for homosexuality because there is nothing to cure. Our sexual orientation and gender identity are not something that requires a cure: homophobia does. Less than half of the United States has outlawed conversion "therapy" practices (Shurka, 2020). There is nothing scientific about the very real torture faced by young LGBTQ+ Americans and young LGBTQ+ individuals worldwide, under the façade of faith.

In *God in Pink,* Namir explores the perspective of being queer and Muslim in a country fraught with its own internal struggles, caused by many external factors, like Iraq. The book is portrayed through the stories of two conflicting characters. Ramy, a gay college student in Iraq, and Ammar, a faith leader in the community. Though fiction, the book allows outsiders to gain the perspective of what it must be like trying to hold onto a faith that does not welcome you. Ammar struggles with helping and guiding someone who has confessed to being gay, but who is still very much a Muslim.

I'm not religious, and like many of my generation, the concept of faith is fluid and can take many forms, but my experiences don't speak for the entire LGBTQ+ community. About 47 percent of LGBTQ+ adults are either "moderately or highly religious. Those who were older, Black or lived in the South were the most likely to be religious," according to Gallup

(Avery, 2020). As you take a deeper look at the demographic and age breakdown of those in the Gallup report, the younger the generation, the queerer. The queerer, the less religious. This might be because for so long religion was not a safe space for us as a community and because of the interpretations made by those literally preaching at the top of these organizations. Simply, there has not been a major representation of our community in these spaces, but that has changed across all faiths as leaders have emerged.

FAITH LEADERS

Mahdia Lynn is the co-founder and executive director of Masjid al-Rabia, an LGBTQ-affirming, anti-racist, pluralist, accessible, and women-centered mosque and Islamic community center in the city of Chicago (Masjid al-Rabia, 2021). She self-identifies as an educator, advocate, and abolitionist who also happens to be a disabled trans woman. In the 2019 Winter edition of *Women in Leadership* magazine, Lynn was featured as their Portrait of a Change-maker. In the magazine, she says that "leadership is not a title or a role you decide for yourself—it is a responsibility, entrusted to you by the communities you serve."

Islam is not the first faith that the public would align with pro-LGBTQ+ teachings. After all, in many of the countries where Islam is the dominant faith, homosexuality is still punishable by death. Mahdia Lynn is leading the narrative to change this perception of Islam. In a conversation on NPR Mahid shares, "I believe that our identities are experiential, not chosen. Faith is a practice, and love is action. I follow the divine voice that calls me to help others—it's the same voice that inspires me to be the best version of myself, and the same voice that calls me to direct action. This is my best me. This is the path set before me to change the world for the better" (Siddiqi, 2019).

Then there is Rev. Naomi Washington-Leapheart, an ordained minister affiliated with the Fellowship of Affirming Ministries and director for Faith-Based and Interfaith Affairs in the Office of the Mayor of the City of Philadelphia (Siddiqi, 2019). She shares, as part of a series on queer faith titled, *"Queer Faith: In Our Own Words,"* her perspective on finding her faith and how she can only be Christian because of, never despite, her queerness and her blackness.

"I find in being black and queer, a thing of beauty, a joy, a strength. A secret cup of gladness. This is a quote by Ossie Davis that I have adapted. I am a black woman minister who is queer and Christian. And as I look back over my life I realized that my blackness and my queerness offered to me, a secret cup of gladness. I would describe this in two ways. The history of black folks in these yet-to-be United States reflects our capacity to transform exile into excellence. Exile is supposed to be a terminal condition. A place where you are sent to die. But for black folks, the wilderness is the very sight of our power. We take what others have called 'scraps' and cook them into an extraordinary meal. Not for other people's consumption, but for our own nourishment. I'm grateful for this inheritance from my ancestors. For this ability to get full and be fed and feed my people, even when others have banished me stonewalled me, ignored me. Called me too much, not enough to disruptive. Not quite a good fit.

And then I put that with what my queerness has given me the audacity to make a love that only needs to be legible to myself. When I came out to myself first. It was really a commitment to releasing my own shame about whether who I am and the way I love could be understood and be celebrated by people who really have no stake in my life. It was finally insisting like Audrey Lord wrote that nothing, I accept about myself can be used against me to diminish me. It was about choosing my own joy my own strength, my own thing of beauty, first, above other choices.

I connect all of these identities to my faith identity because if my faith cannot offer me something in the wilderness moments it isn't worth having. If my faith can not help me to renounce shame, so that I can love myself and love others in a way that is true even if wholly misunderstood, then it isn't worth having. I often wonder if Jesus was and is black and queer. Jesus established a movement in the wild. Multiplying the scraps to feed the whole community. Jesus's way of loving was offensive and got him killed. I wish we had something like Jesus's journals to read. I want to know how his heartache because he's so long to be affirmed to be welcomed in. To have a love of his life. To experience what it is like to be a subject and not an object. I would say that I can only be Christian because I am black and queer. It is through those secret cups of gladness that I can relate to Jesus."

Despite all of the differences, unique intersections, and diversity within the broad queer community, it would be easy to summarize and say that we truly don't have a sense of community, that leading through community is too difficult, and that true LGBTQ+ community leaders can't exist. They may exist in a specific location or through an issue-based point of view, but how do we explain Pride? How do we explain the feeling that many, if not all of us, get when we are doing ordinary things then suddenly see a pride flag sticker on a water bottle or as a bumper sticker? How do we explain the feeling we get when we see a pride flag on the corner of a local business' door, or hung at a local coffee shop? Pride is a community, and we have it year-round.

So, what about community leaders? Where are our Stacey Abrams, Hillary Clinton, Justin Trudeau, Jose Andres, Bill Gates, or Bono? For decades we have had Elton John and RuPaul, but now we have so many leaders that build community and bring us together that I would probably never finish listing them all. While these leaders have surely opened the door for many of the achievements and recognition we now have on a global scale, the next generation, those unheard-of, unrecognized leaders, leaders like you and I, will be the ones to take that next bold step forward towards progress and equality. We all have the potential to be incredible, outspoken, powerful, change-making, resilient leaders for the betterment of not just our community, but the world.

PART III

BUILDING THE COURAGE TO LEAD

13

I'm Coming Out

Ask any LGBTQ+ person and they will tell you that coming out is never a one-time, grandiose event where you are struck with enlightenment and knowledge from all the gays that have existed before you. You are not suddenly handed a mimosa, or Bloody Mary, and welcomed to your first drag brunch where you will live happily ever after with all of your gay friends as long as you all shall live. I hate to break it to you, but when you ask a queer person about their coming out story, it barely scratches the surface of the coming out process. This is because each and every time we meet someone, each and every time we have to write a bio or introduce ourselves to a group, or bring up our partners or significant others, we have to come out again. At some point, all the key players in your life know about the fact that you're not straight and instead of coming out each time to more and more people, you're effectively welcoming or inviting them into your life and into your space. This is when the narrative changes and you get to control the rules of engagement and how the process will occur. Before you can be ready to lead and feel like you're inviting people into your life, you must first come out, over and over again.

THERE IS NOTHING LIKE PARIS

For years I thought I had it all.

Then suddenly, while sitting on the steps of the Paris Opera, I looked out into the street full of people walking in and out of stores, out of the metro, simply going about their day without a care in the world, and I realized I was lost, alone, and confused. The tremendous blow shook the world around me, like one does to a cheap souvenir snow globe you buy at the airport gift shop just to pass time between flights. I just sat there letting it all swirl and clash around me, letting the rush of emotions enter and consume me in only the way a life-changing moment can. I couldn't deny it anymore, this was it, this was me, it had always been me, and it was time to let him out.

I was able to cleverly dodge questions at the dinner table or among even my closest friends and use my education as a shield. I felt the immense pressure to succeed, to not let my family down, to show that our sacrifices were worth it. For years I focused on my education, tremendously exceeding the bare minimum. Add to this immense, internal pressure the external validation of good grades, honors recognitions and constantly being told by my family, peers, and teachers that I was the "responsible one," the one that no one ever had to worry about, and the pressure just kept building to keep on the straight path paved by my successes. I overwhelmed myself in high school with as many AP courses, honor societies, community college classes, and after-school clubs that I could fit into my schedule. There was never a moment where my brain and my attention were not on my academics.

Receiving all this external validation, especially in a state like Texas, with its very clear and explicit societal norms, meant I didn't question anything. I knew that, up until this point, my secretive tactics were winning even though I was only playing myself. For whatever reason, I did know that I needed to get out of Texas... as if this would magically put all the pieces together. Despite the thousands of miles I put between myself and the environment in Texas, nothing changed. Even in college, the pressure remained, pushing me further and further into the life I had fabricated for myself-the life I thought others expected of me. After all, I was the first in my family to go to college and not just any college, but Georgetown University. Neither one of my parents finished high school, and my mother's dad died unable to fully read or write, making me feel as if I had no option but to succeed. However, all the success in the world did not make me a leader. How could I lead anything or anyone if I couldn't first lead myself out of the shadows?

In Paris, an ocean away from the hustle and pressure of Washington and the norms of Texas, it clicked. Often, I found myself walking the streets of Paris the summer of 2015, alone, with no real destination other than a sense of wanting to be there. For years I had imagined what it would be like to live in Paris; yes, I know it's not very original. I wasn't supposed to be in Paris that summer. Instead, I should have been in Lyon, France for the entirety of my junior year of college. I was not good at economics, and it effectively tanked my GPA. Even though I was admitted into the full-year program by the host university, Georgetown didn't let me enroll. So, instead, I was in Paris. But who wouldn't want to spend their summer living there anyway?

Maybe this was the universe's way of telling me to shut up, stop planning, stop worrying, stop hiding, and pretending to be someone I wasn't. Sitting there on the steps of the Paris Opera house watching the sun cast its orange glow on the quintessentially Parisian buildings that line *L'avenue de l'Opera*, it happened. For the first time in my life I uttered, though still internally, those words that for so long had been urging to come out; I'm gay.

On that summer afternoon in Paris of all places, I came out for the first time to the most important person in this never-ending journey—myself.

I lived the rest of that summer in Paris test driving my new identity. I relearned who I was. I stopped closely monitoring how I walked or how I talked. I stopped replaying casual everyday interactions such as checking out at a grocery store or buying a ticket at a museum to see if "I sounded too gay" or if my outfits gave me away as a member of the "others." There were no preconceived notions of who I was or needed to be, and the academic setting while abroad faded into the background. I wasn't worried about exams or assignments, but instead was concerned with which neighborhood I would explore that day or whether it was the bright pink or the saffron yellow bakery that had the best sandwich— the jury is still out. I simply, and openly, could just be me and go about my life in the same way I had done before sitting on those Opera steps. Being surrounded by complete and perfect strangers was incredibly freeing. People think that my time in Paris must have been incredibly sad because I was alone, but it was completely the opposite.

It was perfect.

SIPPING TEA

I left Paris with an incredible and invaluable heirloom souvenir that would have been impossible to find even in the best shops in *Place Vendôme*. Coming out is a never-ending journey. It's a process where we must constantly out ourselves to friends, family, and those with whom we interact. Then suddenly, as those relevant to us know, the tables turn. Instead of coming out, we are bringing them into our world and serve as the encyclopedia of information into the world of the LGBTQ+ community. Coming out and then bringing others in is a lifelong process that requires resilience and leadership.

I returned to Texas that summer and, upon being hit by the cold BBQ-scented Austin airport air, with expert precision, I immediately went back to the closet. I knew who I had always been and was more than happy being my authentic self, but only if no one else knew who I was. So, when I was surrounded by family, friends, and the HEB bakery lady (yes, she played a central role in every birthday party growing up), I instantly put on the straight costume that for so long I considered permanent. Unfortunately, the spaces I was familiar with in Texas never felt safe or right for me to come out.

So I waited, and instead I came out first to my friends back in college during the fall semester of my senior year. The very first person I ever came out to was my friend R. Yes, that is their name, no I'm not hiding their identity as part of some witness protection program. Surprisingly, the summer that I was coming out to myself, they were coming out too.

I received a Facebook message letting me know that they had come out as bisexual. This would be the same way they would later come out as gender non-binary years later. At the time, I was very curious as to how they knew that they felt and identified that way.

Growing up, and even within the LGBTQ+ community, there exists a tremendous level of bi-erasure and biphobia because of misinformation and preconceived notions attached to heterosexual standards of sexuality. Bisexual individuals face constant questioning by those around them asking if "it's just a phase" or asking them to validate their sexuality when they are in heteronormative presenting relationships. I fell into that trap, asking R if they were sure and if they were, how did they know? I tiptoed around my own sexuality to the point where they felt, understandably so, that I was questioning theirs. It resulted probably in the only fight, or one of the very few, that has stayed in my memory.

Like all friends, we eventually got over it. My coming out to them hopefully helped make sense of my line of questioning that summer. R and I sat on a bench in the courtyard by the C&O canal of a restaurant several blocks from the main gates of thirty-seventh and O. We went as far as any Georgetown student would willingly go on foot, right up to Wisconsin Ave. The irony now is that my husband manages a restaurant across from the C&O Canal bench where I first publicly came out. There, R and I sat for what felt like four hours, in the middle of the night. I need to tell them something so important that it couldn't wait until normal hours or be done in the presence of others. To this day, I have no clue what they must have thought I had to share that was so important that I would drag them blocks away from campus, in the middle of the night, but still, they came and sat as I tried to piece together the words.

We walked without a destination. They were fine just walking, just being there as a friend to keep me company as I fumbled around making small talk asking them about their day as if we did not spend an incredible amount of time together. At some point sitting on that bench, I ran out of small talk and had already exhausted all of the other possible topics of what I could possibly need to tell them. No, there wasn't a body hidden somewhere. No, I was not moving suddenly mid-semester the last year of college. I had nothing else to tell them, and the mosquitoes were starting to get to us.

"I'm gay" finally spilled out of my mouth. I had been getting ready for this moment my entire life, but especially since Paris. I knew that after this moment, I couldn't go back. I wouldn't be able to bottle up the words and they escaped out of my mouth, running into the darkness of the September night. Finally sharing that secret with another person made it real, as if I had spoken it into existence. R was supportive, encouraging, and understanding. More than anything, they didn't treat me in the least bit differently, and didn't make the situation awkward. Most of all, unlike the questioning I had for them, they didn't question my coming out.

The next person I told was Nick, one of my housemates. He was very much out and proud in a way that didn't require him to tell you. I admired his courage and strength to be himself. In my eyes he has always been so confident in who he is and didn't try to hide his sexuality. It was always right there on his sleeve if someone cared to look. He openly blended stereotypes with the ambitious and career driven nature of someone pursuing a degree in finance, a subject I have never been able to wrap my head around.

He had become one of my closest friends in college to the point where we knew we could be housemates, but not necessarily roommates—a true sign of friendship and respect. There wasn't a long-drawn, convoluted story that eventually got me to come out to him as I had done so with R. At this point, I needed to let those closest to me know and build support. Nick was also already in that world, and I felt very much like an —insert-your-favorite-baby-animal-here—figuring out how to walk. We were there in our Village A apartment, sitting on the wine-colored couch that had seen better days when I came out to him.

As the words came out of my mouth for the second time in my life, Nick, without missing a beat, got up from the couch, walked over to our fluorescently lit kitchen, and oh so casually asked me, "Do you want some tea?" I was confused by his reaction and quickly nodded, not sure where this was headed.

He responded, "I have this 'celebration' tea that I brought back from Taiwan. I think this calls for some." Just like that, we were celebrating my coming out in the most casual and calm way imaginable—with some tea Nick had brought back from his very own study abroad.

EL CHISME

After that, I can't tell you who I told next or the order of events. It got to the point where my close friends in college and those around me knew I had come out. Eventually, I came out to my mom. I had been trying to do so for some time, but never found the way to casually slip it into a conversation. Some part of me was telling me that I needed to do this in person, face-to-face, but she was thousands of miles away in Texas, and I was in DC. Though I had previously surprised my family by randomly showing up during spring break or some other holiday, it seemed a bit extra to show up in the middle of the fall semester to say "Hi, I'm gay." I was also afraid. I wasn't 100 percent sure what their reaction would be—no LGBTQ+ person, regardless of their age, is ever sure how someone else may react. My mom was also coming to DC for Thanksgiving, but I felt that she needed to know not for her comfort or to protect her from walking into some sort of gay trap when she came to visit, but because I didn't want to live a double life while she visited. I had just escaped the clutches of the closet and I wasn't ready to be forced back into it. After weeks of trying to figure out how to tell her, I finally saw my opportunity.

We were chatting through FaceTime one night towards the end of the week. While we were talking, my mom was distracted with something, probably chisme, that was happening with our family in Mexico. All I knew was that she wasn't completely paying attention and was going back and forth between our video conversation and WhatsApp. This meant that there were moments when the video would pause, and she wasn't looking at the screen. I took that as my chance. I took advantage of the situation.

Carefully, I crafted my text throughout the conversation. It was ready and all I had to do was hit send. When the next pause came up and the screen blurred, I hit send. As my phone made the all-too loud "swoosh" sound, and I stared at the screen anxiously. I waited for what seemed an eternity. I could have just hung up the call and said, "Talk to you later," but I waited. This time the words had hit the ground like a plate in a crowded restaurant. She confusedly said, "*me mandaste un mensaje*" (you texted me).

She read the text, video still paused. I looked at the screen waiting for her face to reappear on camera. I needed to get a sense of her reaction. She could have just as easily hung up and said. "Talk to you later" or she could have sent me to the "chingada," a popular place Mexicans send unwanted nonsense.

Her face said it all; She was overwhelmed. It was too much to process so quickly. From the moment I sent the text, my mind went cold. Do you know the sensation you get when you eat peppermint? Where your mouth is both cold and numb? When breathing hurts? Well, that is exactly what coming out feels like. Numbing.

I don't remember if it was at that moment that she asked if I was sure and how I knew, or if this conversation happened the next day, but I knew there would be more time to talk when she visited in a few weeks. What I do remember, and what I knew at that very moment, was that I wanted that call to be over. I had just come out to my mom over FaceTime and was tremendously overwhelmed, but I had also intentionally planned to go out with my friends that night. This would be a distraction and defrost from what had just transpired over the phone. Thank you, technology. So, I said, "I have to go. There's a party, my friends are waiting." I said goodbye and told her we could talk later.

There was a part of me that knew that this had opened the door for my mom to tell the rest of the family. After all, the *chisme* was strong and being *chismosos* runs in the family. At the same time, I wish I would have been able to control how and when I came out to my brother and sister, but especially my dad. For better or for worse it was out.

NEW YEAR, NEW ME!

On New Year's Eve, 2015, less than six months after coming out to myself and to those closest to me, I chose to come out publicly. With a rather lengthy and bilingual post on Facebook, I didn't just come out of the closet, but set fire to it and left that mess behind. By doing so, I was eliminating the possibility of ever being able to go back in the closet; it was now on the internet forever, much like my questionable hair choices. At the same time, I was making sure that I didn't feel the need to come out again. If you knew me from when I was pretending and choosing to be straight and cared enough about me, you would receive the initial "shocking" news through social media along with the millions of other "New Year, New Me" posts. If you met me in 2016 and beyond, then you met Jonathan. Unvarnished, unfiltered, and unapologetic.

"Okay its long but important:

[I] made myself a promise at this time last year that 2015 was dedicated to "me, myself, and I" and I think to myself now that we have come a long way. These past three-hundred and sixty-five days have been filled with incredible opportunities that have made the setbacks insignificant. Looking back, not only am I halfway done with my senior year at Georgetown and have lived in Paris for two months, but I really did put myself first. 2016 will be an even greater year because I've discovered how truly happy and confident I can be when I'm completely and utterly myself without holding back, which includes being gay. Yes, I am gay and no there is no way you knew, because until recently I didn't even know, so get over it. So I'm making a promise to myself now that I will no longer doubt myself, that I will be obnoxiously confident and incredibly happy not just for 2016, but for the rest of my life. During these past several months I have realized how truly fortunate I am to have been given such an incredibly supportive and loving family, and friends who are unquestionably by my side, and I realize that unfortunately some little kids, teens, and even adults don't have this opportunity. I am still very much me. No, I haven't magically changed overnight. Whatever may be your opinion of me, hold on to it because there is nothing holding me back this time around the sun, remember it's a leap year, so watch out. I'm going to make 2016 my best year yet!" – Facebook December 2015.

Constantly having to come out, or invite in, and validate one's existence reinforces the identity of members of the

LGBTQ+ community. For some of us, we recognize our authentic selves immediately the first time we can discern ourselves in the mirror. Others take years, even decades to shed their hard exteriors built up by years of stereotypes and affirmations. However, along the journey to authenticity, this process makes us stronger, more confident, more social, and yes, ready to lead. Living authentically gives LGBTQ+ community members a sense of confidence unlike any other. Those of us who have the privilege to live as our authentic selves also have the responsibility to lead and pave the path forward for future generations and make welcoming spaces for others to come out. We must be leaders; we must be out to lead.

Living authentically, I have discovered how much my queerness impacted who I have become. For most of my life, I thought it was my intelligence and academic excellence that molded me. That bubble was promptly popped when I started college. Everyone was smarter than me and more prepared. Honestly, I was naive to think that I could compete with generations of family wealth and degrees for a spot at the top of the academic ladder. Let me let you in on a little secret, I graduated in the bottom five people of my undergraduate class, but I was the proudest and happiest person on commencement day. Coming out my senior year of college saved me from the academic disappointment I had become to my closeted self. I saw how my resilience built through my queer identity had always been my driving force to excel and lead.

14

The Rainbow Road Ahead

———

Knowing where we come from is critical if we want to be able to see where we are going. If we want to be able to shape our future, we need to understand how we are going to ensure that we don't just get there, but that we don't take steps back.

THE QUEER VOTE

There are an estimated nine million LGBTQ+ registered voters as of the 2020 election (Mallory, 2019). To put that into perspective, if all the queers suddenly found themselves living in one state, we would be the tenth most populated state in the country right up there between North Carolina and Michigan (Census, 2021). Remember, this is just from those who are registered to vote. There is an estimated 21 percent of LGBTQ+ adults who are not registered (Mallory, 2019), and that brings our population closer to states like Ohio or Georgia. It should come as no surprise then, that our community is incredibly diverse, though it's also not a monolith. We may traditionally be a liberal powerhouse voting bloc, 50 percent identify as Democrat compared to 38 percent of non-queer voters, but that only describes half of us (Mallory, 2019).

Breaking down the LGBTQ+ vote even more, the Williams Institute at the UCLA School of Law concludes that out of the nine million registered LGBTQ+ voters, 15 percent identify as Republican, and 22 percent identify as Independent. The remaining 13 percent either identify with another party or weren't truly sure which party they best identified with. Demographically, our community is just as diverse with 22 percent identifying as Latinx, 13 percent identifying as Black, 4 percent of other races or multiracial, and the remaining 61 percent are white. While nearly 40 percent of Queer voters are voters of color, only 30 percent of non-queer voters identify as belonging to a community of color.

While clearly the queer community is not a monolith, we aren't going anywhere. It is estimated that nearly 50 percent of the LGBTQ+ voters are under the age of thirty-four and, by contrast, only 20 percent of the queer vote is over the age of fifty-five (Mallory, 2019). However, we must take into consideration that this number is likely higher, but we will never get the actual number. This generation was the one who fought in the first and second World War, lived through the Great Depression, and lived during a time where being anything other than a "red-blooded" American was met with some level of suspicion. It's unfortunate that we are likely never to know the stories of our queer elders simply because our community did not have a safe way to leave a record of that generation.

The true power of the queer vote has only come to the foreground of the political landscape and political decision-makers since the turn of the twenty-first century, but that also has a lot to do with the growing number of out LGBTQ+ individuals. Politicians, businesses, and society at large have taken note and are paying attention.

Since 2017, the queer population was estimated to be around 4.5 percent of the total US adult population (Jones, 2021). However, as the Gen-Z generation has reached voting age, it is estimated that one in six identifies as LGBT with the majority identifying as bisexual. According to Gallup "more than half of LGBT adults identify as bisexual. About a quarter say they are gay, with about 10 percent identifying as lesbian and 10 percent as transgender. The remainder elects another non-heterosexual preference or term to describe their sexual orientation, such as queer or same-gender-loving" (Jones, 2021).

This has fundamentally changed the national identity of the LGBTQ+ community with an estimate that now 5.6 percent of the adult population is a member of the community (Jones, 2021). When you look deeper and realize that the majority of the Gen-Zers, born between 1997 and 2012, are still under the age of eighteen, and therefore not part of this study, means that the number is only going to increase as they reach voting age.

Each generation would, on paper and in a purely academic sense, appear to be getting "gayer" according to the most recent research by Gallup. In the traditionalist generation, of those born before 1946, only 1.3 percent identify as LGBT, while only 2 percent of the Baby Boomer generation (1946-1964) and 3.8 percent of Generation X (1965-1980) are part of the LGBT community. When you begin to look at millennials, my generation, born between 1981 and 1996, there is a tripling of the percentage of the LGBTQ+ population from 3.8 percent to 9.1 percent. At the same time, there is an almost equally as large part of the population that had no opinion. By the time you get to Gen-Z, you have an almost sixteen percent of the generation identifying as LGBTQ+ and 5.2 percent of the population having no opinion.

It is interesting to take a look at the population without an opinion about their sexuality. A staunch straight/heterosexual individual, especially those who are opposed to LGBTQ+ rights, would automatically identify as such. Having no opinion about your sexuality can mean that you don't care for labels or that the labels provided by Gallup—Lesbian, Gay, Bisexual, and Transgender—don't apply. There is no good understanding, at least that I have found, that adequately captures those who may identify as Queer or Gender-Nonbinary.

Many studies, policies, and institutions stop at the "T" in LGBTQ+. The Q can stand for Queer, as it most often does, and or questioning. The Gay Lesbian Alliance Against Defamation (GLAAD) has a super useful media reference guide, or glossary, of terms for the community. There, it expands on the term Queer which, I believe, captures the limitations by Gallup at adequately capturing a snapshot of our community.

According to GLAAD, Queer is "an adjective used by some people, particularly younger people, whose sexual orientation is not exclusively heterosexual (e.g. queer person, queer woman). Typically, for those who identify as queer, the terms lesbian, gay, and bisexual are perceived to be too limiting and/or fraught with cultural connotations they feel don't apply to them. Some people may use queer, or more commonly gender-queer, to describe their gender identity and/or gender expression (see non-binary and/or gender-queer below). Once considered a pejorative term, queer has been reclaimed by some LGBT people to describe themselves; however, it is not a universally accepted term even within the LGBT community. When Q is seen at the end of LGBT, it typically means queer and, less often, questioning."

Then there is the "+." If included, it is often there to capture the additional members of the community. Often this to the IP2SAA part of the acronym not so common in our day-to-day lexicon. This refers to intersex, pansexual, two spirit, asexual and androgynous. Quickly you can start to realize that there isn't a standard after the "T" and, unfortunately, this is as far as a large part of the globe has gone to agree on what is and isn't a part of the community. In Europe, and many international organizations, however, the acronym is LGBTI to include the intersex community. The acronym says more about where you live and the audience than one might expect.

2035

So, where is the community headed? Frankly, wherever we want. From the Oval Office to the corner office, from leading within our hyper-local community to leading on the global stage. We are coming out of the closets, and into the streets.

The New Republic asked this very question of LGBTQ+ activists in 2015. "What will gay culture look like in 2035." Kera Bolonik, Editor in Chief of *Dame Magazine,* said, "In 20 years, my hope, at least, is that we don't assume our kids are heterosexual from the moment they're born and that we don't use words like 'tolerance' because really, it's intolerable" (Chee, 2015). In almost ten years since this comment, it seems like that may finally be catching on. Fewer people are assuming their kids will be heterosexual, but the assumption that their kids may grow up to be queer isn't accepted.

Now, as a proud Guncle, or gay uncle, and one of the oldest cousins in my family, especially as the gay one, there is no way that I would assume the sexuality of my niece. If you love someone, that shouldn't matter. The funny thing is, we, as a society, assume that kids will automatically be heterosexual and cisgender, and then we are shocked when that's not the case. Humans don't like to be wrong and more often the hate towards LGBTQ+ individuals stems from having your view of another human's life shattered. Society is the one that is setting us to fail; to hate. We are constantly shown images of what life should be like. You know, the family of four with a single-family home, a white picket fence, in a middle-class neighborhood, and the golden retriever? That's the stereotype. Take the notion that on a person's wedding day you will see a bride walk down the aisle, or a groom standing at the altar. Well, there was no bride at my wedding and we both walked down separate aisles.

Kera also says that by 2035, "in terms of things 'queer,' the discourse is changing at a fast clip right now. Gay and lesbian would seem, to those outside the mainstream, old hat—'homonormative,' if that's a thing" (Chee, 2015). Similar to the concept of assuming that a baby will be straight, we often assume that if they aren't straight, they will be gay or lesbian because of the gender binary that has for so long dominated our conversation. First, we are assuming they must choose and that they won't be attracted to both, in a binary sense, genders. #BiErasure. Secondly, we are assuming that the world will forever operate on the gender binary which, as already discussed, we don't have a good understanding of, but is likely to include a vast swath of the population without an opinion in Gallups polls.

For some, such as Ira Silverberg, former literary director to the National Endowment for the Art, has some fears about where the queer movement may be by 2035. "My thought is that by 2035 the mainstreaming of queer life in America will be so complete that our concerns will turn to historical preservation, and the documentation of harder times and battles. Well, some of us will have those concerns. Many will simply take advantage of the freedom they have, never knowing what we fought for so they could have it. I could go on about how important I think it will be to remember and highlight the work of the lost generation. AIDS decimated our community, and our creative community was especially hard hit. Many of those artists were the same ones on the front lines of the culture war. May their work be sought out, brought back, and made available for future generations" (Chee, 2015).

The LGBTQ+ community can thank Trump—I know I cringed too—for the fact that clearly our fight is not over. In 2015, many of us expected Hillary Clinton to shatter that glass ceiling and become our first woman president. Trump was a major wake-up call, making us all realize that we can't take our rights and freedoms for granted because you never know who might get elected next. Certainly, we must make sure that we don't forget about the struggles faced by pioneers of the LGBTQ+ rights movement. We can't forget how we lost an entire generation to AIDS. My generation may have taken many of our hard-won freedoms for granted, but I don't think we are anywhere close to our lives and our stories being part of mainstream culture. Just look at the award shows that have snubbed major LGBTQ+ artists and shows and the number of times our stories have been told through the gaze and fetishization of those outside of our community.

By 2035, maybe as a global community, we will understand that there are bigger problems than who loves who and what happens behind closed doors. Hannah Doress, a cofounder of Shore Up Marin, says, "You have to take inequality and climate-sea level rise into account. A foot or more in sea levels will impact many of our LGBTI traditional places of safety—NYC, Boston, San Francisco. And if we let inequality continue rising, it will undermine the economic gains LGBTIs have made, particularly in these safer areas" (Chee, 2015). Come to think of it, the queer "megacities" are located primarily along the coast – another possible thesis research topic right there – and our communities are directly at risk of being displaced. Climate change is a national security risk that will impact everyone regardless of their sexual orientation or gender identity, but it may impact the LGBTQ+ community disproportionately.

Clearly, this is from a US perspective. There are still eleven countries around the world where the death penalty is a possibility for being gay, with six of those implementing it. Iran, Nigeria, Saudi Arabia, Somalia, and Yemen have acted upon this law, while Afghanistan, Brunei, Mauritania, Pakistan, Qatar, and the United Arab Emirates, have the death penalty as a legal possibility, according to the Human Dignity Trust. Globally, seventy-two nations still criminalize homosexuality, and fifteen have specific national laws that target gender expression, so-called "disguise" laws. The only thing being disguised, and not very well, is homophobia. Yes, in many of these countries the moment isn't right to combat these laws; as has been mentioned, the hearts and minds aren't ready to be won, resulting in the flight of the LGBTQ+ community to safer locations. While it is not our place, especially from the American point of view, to go to these nations and demand equality, we can do our part at home to influence the conversation abroad.

Each one of us has a brick to place on the rainbow road towards equality. We can all do our part at home to confront homophobia when we see it and make sure that we aren't passive bystanders when we see it in the world. By coming out, when and if safe to do so, we can begin to reshape the future by taking control of our narrative. Simply existing is an act of resistance. Know that it truly does get better and that you're not alone.

The path ahead isn't an easy one, but we are used to it. We are used to rising from the ashes time and time again despite attempts to stamp us out of history and criminalize us for simply existing. As we move forward, we aren't just meant to take up space, but it is desperately needed. We bring a wealth of knowledge, a unique perspective, and the ability to lead through lived experiences, which has instilled in us the resilience to take on tomorrow's challenges today.

15

Out to Lead

—

From the birth of humanity, lesbians, gays, bisexuals, transgender, intersex, two-spirit, and queer individuals have existed. Humans may have put names and labels, but diverse sexual orientations and gender identities have always existed in nature. At some point, we let certain teachings take over how we viewed the world, and this became the norm. We began to see the world in black and white —mainly as just white—and began to hide and diminish color. Humanity for so long has lived in this binary. Right or wrong, up or down, male or female. Imagine how much further along we would be as a civilization if we would have embraced the diversity of thought, race, sexual orientation, and gender identity from the start? If, at the moment of the inception of 'us versus them,' some brave individual or community would have stood up and said, "wait a minute!"

Between the ancient Greeks and the early 1900s, there is an almost three-thousand-year gap of queer history as told by our perspective. There are plenty of mentions of how we weren't allowed to exist through the laws set in place and the practices put on the books to try to erase our presence, some of which are still in place today. Just as we began to see the rise in elected officials in the United States and the potential for a shift towards normalizing our identity as leaders, our community was hit by the AIDS pandemic. We lost thousands, and an entire generation, due to the inaction by governments around the world to put the money behind the research for a cure simply because this was a "gay" problem. Together, we have come out of thousands of years of inaction to be the formidable political, financial, and cultural force we are today. We are demanding, no longer asking, to be respected, seen, and included.

Normalizing our existence and being visible, in whatever capacity that we can, will be how we create a rainbow wave that can ripple across all societies. We aren't here to convert everyone towards homosexuality, though I'm sure some think we may be out here holding a secret meeting on how to spread the queer agenda. (They do on Saturday mornings; it's called brunch.) More than anything, we don't want our sexuality or gender identity to be shocking or a point of controversy. LGBTQ+ people want to live authentically, and we don't want our existence to be threatened. Going to the grocery store or sitting on a park bench shouldn't always have to be an act of resistance.

Today's generation, and future generations, may have an easier time finding the words and the strength to be out, but that doesn't mean that being queer today is any easier than it was five or fifty years ago. Discrimination towards transgender individuals is at an all-time high around the globe. Especially in the United States, laws are proposed every single day to make the lives of the transgender community incredibly difficult. While social media has allowed thousands to find resources, it has become an increasingly toxic and dangerous place for our community as it has become easier for homophobia to hide behind a screen and preach hatred.

The fight for equality hasn't ended just because we achieved marriage equality. It has just begun and will continue with the hope that one day every member of our community is truly equal and respected across these yet-to-be united nations.

To some extent yes, the population may be getting queerer and queerer, but there is probably a larger cultural shift happening. Compared to past generations, we millennials, and Gen-Z, now have the language to express our identities beyond simply homosexual and queer, which have for so long had negative connotations. We can go beyond the heteronormative male and female and beyond the homonormative gay and lesbian. With this, also comes the ability to live authentically instead of upholding some sort of societal norms. The internet and social media have undoubtedly helped many a baby queer take one of several online quizzes to answer the age-old question "am I gay?"

Let me tell you, if you googled "Am I gay?" you're gay.

After coming out, I walked around the streets of Paris. I just walked without a real destination, and for the first time in my life, the phrase "It's not about the destination, it's the journey" actually made sense. I was probably blasting a combination of *This Summer* by Maroon 5 and *Cool for the Summer* by Demi Lovato... very appropriate in my opinion. Looking back, I walked so many miles that summer throughout

Paris, learning that city like the back of my hand. To this day, it's probably one of the cities that I best know how to get around. I didn't have internet service on my phone, so I had to take screenshots of the routes ahead of time and hope it would help. I walked everywhere. That night, I knew I had to go back home, but I didn't just make a beeline for it; I was free, and I could go wherever. Thanks to technology, and my passion for taking terrible photos, I can essentially re-trace those steps.

Starting on the Paris Opera steps, I walked down *Rue de la Paix*, or Peace Street, towards the *Jardin des Tuileries*, cutting right through the middle of *Place Vendôme*, which is where some of the world's top luxury brands and the famous Ritz hotel calls home. Walking down the cobblestone streets, I eventually reached the gardens—an extension of the Louvre. There was a fair, so I stopped and took a picture. This was before night mode so you can imagine how these pictures look. I continued to walk the perimeter of the park towards *Place de la Concorde* where I took several more awful photos. These photos are now precious, capturing my first moments after coming out. I now realize how truly privileged I am to have experienced it with such a sense of happiness and fantasy.

At this point it was late, and it was a Wednesday, which meant I had class the next morning. At Place de *la Concorde*, I walked into the metro and took a picture with the tiles that seem to resemble some sort of word search. Heading home on the metro that night I felt different. Truly I felt lighter, as if I no longer had to carry this lie—a burden—with me everywhere. It took several months after to fully get rid of the disguise, but that summer I got rid of most of it and only kept the glasses. If it worked for Superman as a disguise, then it worked for me to protect my identity in those most vulnerable moments. Eventually, I would toss those too.

Since coming out, my life has changed in so many incredible ways. I met my husband, Juan, by the end of my senior year of college and I proposed in New York City in front of the Alice in Wonderland statue in Central Park; I tried, and failed, to use the Mad Hatter line of "Have I gone mad?" We got married in 2019 in Washington DC and had one of the most amazing nights of my life with our family, both chosen and biological. While the pictures of that night were incredible, they will never do justice to the love, support, and pure joy felt by everyone in attendance.

What I have achieved thus far would have never been possible without coming out. The confidence, and most importantly, the resilience I have developed to confront all that life may throw my way is only possible because I am gay. Coming to terms with my sexuality and identity was pivotal for me to be able to breathe and take it all in. It also opened my eyes to the challenges I had unconsciously chosen not to confront. In so many ways, coming out saved me, and despite whatever friends I may have lost, rejections I may have faced, and obstacles placed in my way, I wouldn't change it for anything in the world.

Being out and living with pride means owning your unique truths (O.U.T.) and living passionately, resiliently, intentionally, defiantly, and empathetically (P.R.I.D.E.). Individually, we all have to reach that moment, but there is a community waiting for you once you're ready. From coming out, to being a leader, there isn't a huge jump if you're willing to own your unique truths. Leaders must be able to realize that they are, in fact, leaders. Realizing that the only barrier left for queer leaders to lead is just owning it is fundamental.

Queer leadership starts when we realize that we are the ones who have the power to tell our own stories. There are moments that will be forever engraved into the forefront of our minds because they changed our lives forever. These may be incredibly positive events such as being the first in your family to graduate from college, finding your life partner, landing that job that is more than just a paycheck, or coming out. In the same way, these events can leave a mark because of how difficult they were: almost being kicked out of college because you weren't able to pay for it or the anxiety and fear caused by making the conscious decision to be out and proud.

Whether it's focusing on your academic life to the point where you, intentionally, had no time for a "girlfriend" in high school, being a trailblazer for your family and turning your dream of going to college into a reality, or deciding to go into a non-traditional career for an educated Latinx, the spotlight is there. But it's there to call attention to you, to destroy the barriers you cleverly constructed and pierce past the façade you've created to protect yourself from your true self.

LGBTQ+ individuals already have the skills to be resilient. We know that life is complicated because we have lived that each and every day. Collectively, we choose to focus on the positive and not just the negative. Just look at the month of June, at how much pride comes out that month. Yes, it should also serve as an understanding that the first pride was a riot, but it is also a moment to look around at our community, be happy, and realize we've made it this far. Widely, the LGBTQ+ community is incredibly honest with themselves, one another, and even those outside the community. We live our truth and keep it real every single day.

We've been here, and we will continue to be here for generations to come. We won't only see progress continue, but we will make sure it happens.

So, own the attention that the pitch of your voice may bring, and the attention that the confidence you exude when walking down the street gains. Own your identity, your sexuality, and take up space. Do it because, at that moment, you're free. In these moments you show how resilient you are and how much power there is in your existence. Realize the shoulders that you stand on and the struggles that our community has faced for you to be here, where you were meant to be.

Maybe that's what sets leaders in the community apart. We aren't happy with a rainbow flag or gay character having a part-time role on TV. We want more. We want to take up space and cause good trouble, uplift, and bring our community along, and not forget that we stand on the shoulders of a few generations of leaders that came before.

We must be out to lead for those who can't.

Meet the Author

Mexican made, Texas-raised, & DC educated, Jonathan Dromgoole is a community leader focused on increasing representation for the Latinx & LGBTQ+ community through policy & public service. Jonathan is a first-generation double graduate of Georgetown University (SFS '16 & MPP '19). Jonathan's professional & personal achievements have focused on social good & people-centered policies that enhance diverse representation from international development practices to local activism. He lives with his husband, Juan, & their two dogs in Northern Virginia.

Learn more about Jonathan and stay connected on social media. Simply scan below!

Mil Gracias

———

THERE ARE SO MANY PEOPLE WHO I WOULD LIKE TO THANK. TO THOSE WHO SUPPORTED AND BELIEVED IN ME EVERY STEP OF THE WAY, BUT ALSO TO THOSE WHO DOUBTED, MADE FUN OF, AND CRITICIZED ME... THANKS TO YOU, I AM RESILIENT. Thank you to those queer leaders who came before me to shatter glass ceilings, throw open closet doors, and create space for our community to thrive. Whether or not your contribution made headlines or the pages of this book, your impact on our community is felt every day.

Thank you to those who helped make sure that this book went from an idea to a draft, and from my laptop to your home.

Brandi Acosta
Tyler Adamson
Cristina Araujo
Sevda Aysel
Rachel Becker
Molly Bernick

Heidy Betances
Juan Carlos Bordas
Karinna Bordas
Pablo Bordas
Hannah Borja
Mariana Brazao

Rachel Brooks
James Cameron
Christian Camacho
Cathy Caminero
Sarah Campbell
Sheryll Cashin
Jesse Catir
Alexander Cintron
Christopher Concepcion
Gabriella Cooper
Victoria Coy
Colleen Daly
Nathalie Denham
Laura Dickinson
Barbara Dromgoole
Brandon Dromgoole
Juan Dromgoole
John Dromgoole
Olga Dromgoole
Sabrina Duff
Matthew Finch
Alessandra Fix
Isabella Fix
Jamie Fullerton
Valerie Gonzales
Matthew Hellman
Nancy Hernandez
Mauricio Hernandez
Valerie Herrera
Chantelle Johnson
Laura-Claire Jones
Ryan Kaminski

Haseeb Khatri
Ofelia Knapp
Eric Koester
Eliza Lopez
Brenda Lozano
Chris Luna
Brian Marroquin
Leopoldo Martinez
Paul Miller
Pablo Moulden
Heather Norcross
Darnell Nuñez
Alhelí Partida
Chantal Portillo
Cristina Primavera
Rachel Reibach
Damaris Reyes
Laura Rodriguez
Cristal Rodriguez
Sofia Rosales
Gretchen Ruck
Marco Sanchez
Suzanne Simon
Bettina Stern
Patricia Stupp
Joshua Teitelbaum
Caragan Thiel
Marisela Torres Smith
Kirsten Tuberville
Sari Valdes
Gisselle Villegas
Sitara Weerakoon

Nick Werner
Brooke Wolfe
Evan Wolfson
Toddchelle Young

Appendix

INTRODUCTION

"Building Your Resilience." American Psychological Association. American Psychological Association, 2012. https://www.apa.org/topics/resilience.

Flores, Andrew, and Charles Gossett. "Analysis | 11 Openly LGBTQ Lawmakers Will Take Their Seats in the next Congress. That's a Record in Both Numbers and Diversity." The Washington Post. WP Company, November 30, 2020. https://www.washingtonpost.com/politics/2020/11/30/11-lgbtq-legislators-will-take-their-seats-next-congress-largest-most-diverse-group-ever/.

Giardina, Henry. "America Is About to Elect the Queerest Congress in History." them. Them., November 10, 2020. https://www.them.us/story/america-is-about-to-elect-the-queerest-congress-in-history.

Mayo Clinic Staff. "How to Build Resiliency." Mayo Clinic. Mayo Foundation for Medical Education and Research, October

27, 2020. https://www.mayoclinic.org/tests-procedures/resilience-training/in-depth/resilience/art-20046311.

RuPaul's Drag Race. "If You Can't Love Yourself, How in the Hell You Gonna Love Somebody Else? Can I Get an Amen? - @RuPaul #DragRace #Wisdom." Twitter. Twitter, February 5, 2013. https://twitter.com/rupaulsdragrace/status/298626899360505856?lang=en.

Victory Fund. "2020 - Explore a Year in LGBTQ History: Pride & Progress." Explore a Year in LGBTQ History | Pride & Progress, 2021. https://www.prideandprogress.org/years/2020#adjusting-to-campaigning-during-a-pandemic-hundreds-of-lgbtq-candidates-win.

Victory Institute. Out for America. LGBTQ Victory Institute, December 9, 2019. https://outforamerica.org/.

CHAPTER 1: WE'RE HERE, WE'RE QUEER!

"A Timeline of HIV and AIDS." HIV.gov. US Department of Health and Human Services, April 8, 2021. https://www.hiv.gov/hiv-basics/overview/history/hiv-and-aids-timeline.

HRC. "HIV and the LGBTQ Community." HRC. Accessed May 22, 2021. https://www.hrc.org/resources/hrc-issue-brief-hiv-aids-and-the-lgbt-community.

Schwartz, John. "Austin, Proud of Eccentricity, Loses a Favorite." The New York Times. The New York Times, March 10, 2012. https://www.nytimes.com/2012/03/10/us/austin-proud-of-eccentricity-loses-a-favorite.html.

Texas House of Representatives. "Texas House of Representatives."
State of Texas Flag. Accessed May 22, 2021. https://house.texas.
gov/about-us/state-of-texas-flag/.

Texas State Preservation Board. "Capitol Myths and Legends."
Texas State Preservation Board, 2021. https://tspb.texas.gov/
prop/tc/tc-history/myths-legends/index.html.

"Youth Homelessness." The Trevor Project, July 9, 2018. https://
www.thetrevorproject.org/get-involved/trevor-advocacy/
homelessness/.

CHAPTER 2: OUR HISTORY, OR LACK OF

BBC. "Homosexuality: The Countries Where It Is Illegal to Be Gay."
BBC News. BBC Reality Check Team, May 12, 2021. https://
www.bbc.com/news/world-43822234.

"Bostock v. Clayton County." Oyez. Accessed May 22, 2021. https://
www.oyez.org/cases/2019/17-1618.

Davison, James. "Mad About the Boy." The Guardian. Guardian
News and Media, November 10, 2007. https://www.theguard-
ian.com/books/2007/nov/10/history.society.

Desk, India Today Web. "Homosexuality in Ancient India:
10 Instances." India Today, July 10, 2018. https://www.
indiatoday.in/india/story/10-instances-of-homosexuali-
ty-among-lgbts-in-ancient-india-1281446-2018-07-10.

Diamant, Jeff. "The Countries with the 10 Largest Christian
Populations and the 10 Largest Muslim Populations." Pew

Research Center. Pew Research Center, April 1, 2019. https://
www.pewresearch.org/fact-tank/2019/04/01/the-countries-
with-the-10-largest-christian-populations-and-the-10-larg-
est-muslim-populations/.

Hirshman, Linda R. *Victory: the Triumphant Gay Revolution*. London: Harper Perennial, 2018.

Kane, Kavita. "Storytelling: LGBT Themes in Hindu
Mythology." The Indian Express, July 14, 2020.
https://indianexpress.com/article/parenting/blog/
storytelling-lgbt-themes-in-hindu-mythology-5273332/.

Kurtzleben, Danielle. "Gay Couples More Educated, High-
er-Income Than Heterosexual Couples." US News & World
Report. US News & World Report, March 1, 2013. https://www.
usnews.com/news/articles/2013/03/01/gay-couples-more-ed-
ucated-higher-income-than-heterosexual-couples#:~:tex-
t=Around%2046%20percent%20of%20people,incomes%20
for%20same%2Dsex%20households.

"Lawrence v. Texas." Oyez. Accessed May 22, 2021. https://www.
oyez.org/cases/2002/02-102.

Library of Congress. "Treaty of Paris of 1898." Treaty of Paris of
1898 - The World of 1898: The Spanish-American War (His-
panic Division, Library of Congress). Accessed May 23, 2021.
https://www.loc.gov/rr/hispanic/1898/treaty.html.

Masci, David, Elizabeth Sciupac, and Michael Lipka. "Gay Marriage Around the World." Pew Research Center's Religion &

Public Life Project, October 28, 2019. https://www.pewforum. org/fact-sheet/gay-marriage-around-the-world/.

Mendelsohn, Daniel, and Rebecca Mead. "How Gay Was Sappho?" The New Yorker, March 9, 2015. https://www.newyorker.com/ magazine/2015/03/16/girl-interrupted.

"Obergefell v. Hodges." Oyez. Accessed May 22, 2021. https://www. oyez.org/cases/2014/14-556.

The Department of State Bulletin. United States: Office of Public Communication, Bureau of Public Affairs, 1981.

PBS. "Stonewall Uprising." PBS. Public Broadcasting Service, June 9, 2020. https://www.pbs.org/wgbh/americanexperience/films/ stonewall/.

Plato. "Symposium." Translated by Benjamin Jowett. The Internet Classics Archive | Symposium by Plato. MIT . Accessed May 23, 2021. http://classics.mit.edu/Plato/symposium.html.

Prager, Sarah. "In Han Dynasty China, Bisexuality Was the Norm." JSTOR Daily. JSTOR, June 10, 2020. https://daily.jstor.org/ in-han-dynasty-china-bisexuality-was-the-norm/.

Reuters Staff. "Timeline: Marriage and Homosexual Rights in France." Reuters. Thomson Reuters, January 13, 2013. https:// www.reuters.com/article/us-france-gaymarriage-time/ timeline-marriage-and-homosexual-rights-in-france-idUS- BRE90C0AO20130113.

Schneider, Mike. "Gay Marriages Rise 5 Years after Supreme Court Ruling." AP NEWS. Associated Press, September 17, 2020. https://apnews.com/article/census-2020-us-news-ap-top-news-courts-marriage-587455c1d71f6363b2d272253f916b88.

Tanley, John D. "Europe: The Enlightenment." glbtq encyclopedia . glbtq inc, 2004. http://www.glbtqarchive.com/ssh/europe_ enlightenment_S.pdf.

Taylor, Adam. "What Was the First Country to Legalize Gay Marriage?" The Washington Post. WP Company, June 26, 2015. https://www.washingtonpost.com/news/worldviews/ wp/2015/06/26/what-was-the-first-country-to-legalize-gay-marriage/.

Williams, Lena. "200,000 March in Capital to Seek Gay Rights and Money for AIDS." *The New York Times*, October 12, 1987, 47290 edition, sec. A1.

Zhang, Yuxin. "China's Misunderstood History of Gay Tolerance." The Diplomat. The Diplomat, June 22, 2015. https://thediplomat. com/2015/06/chinas-misunderstood-history-of-gay-tolerance/.

CHAPTER 3: BEFORE PRIDE THERE WAS PREJUDICE

Broich, John. "How the Nazis Destroyed the First Gay Rights Movement." The Conversation, July 4, 2017. https://theconversation.com/how-the-nazis-destroyed-the-first-gay-rights-movement-80354.

Djajic-Horváth, Aleksandra. "Magnus Hirschfeld." Encyclopædia Britannica. Encyclopædia Britannica, inc., May 10, 2021. https://www.britannica.com/biography/Magnus-Hirschfeld.

"Exec. Order No. 10450 Fed. Reg. 2489." National Archives and Records Administration. National Archives and Records Administration, April 27, 1953. https://www.archives.gov/federal-register/codification/executive-order/10450.html.

Fisher, Marshall Jon. "A Terrible Splendor: Three Extraordinary Men, a World Poised for War, and the Greatest Tennis Match Ever Played." United Kingdom: Crown, 2009.

Foreman, Adam. "Coming Out Under Fire: The Story of Gay and Lesbian Service Members: The National WWII Museum: New Orleans." The National WWII Museum | New Orleans. The National World War II Museum, June 24, 2020. https://www.nationalww2museum.org/war/articles/gay-and-lesbian-service-members.

Giles, Geoffrey J. "Why Bother about Homosexuals? : Homophobia and Sexual Politics in Nazi Germany." United States Holocaust Memorial Museum. United States Holocaust Memorial Museum, 2002. https://collections.ushmm.org/search/catalog/bib76214.

Gleason, James. "LGBT History: The Lavender Scare." NGLCC, October 3, 2017. https://www.nglcc.org/blog/lgbt-history-lavender-scare.

Haynes, Suyin, and Video by Arpita Aneja. "History You Didn't Learn About the Anti-Gay Lavender Scare." Time.

Time, December 22, 2020. https://time.com/5922679/lavender-scare-history/.

Heger, Heinz. *The Men with the Pink Triangle: the True Life-and-Death Story of Homosexuals in the Nazi Death Camps.* Los Angeles, CA: Alyson, 2010.

"Henry Gerber." Chicago LGBT Hall of Fame, 2019. http://chicagolgbthalloffame.org/gerber-henry/.

HRC. "About." About - HRC. HRC. Accessed May 24, 2021. https://www.hrc.org/about.

Keehnen, Owen. "Lili Elbe." Edited by Victor Salvo. Legacy Project Chicago, 2020. https://legacyprojectchicago.org/person/lili-elbe.

Lucero, Louis. "Memories of That Night at the Stonewall Inn, From Those Who Were There." The New York Times. The New York Times, June 16, 2019. https://www.nytimes.com/2019/06/16/us/revisiting-stonewall-memories-history.html.

Marhoefer, Laurie. Sex and the Weimar Republic: German Homosexual Emancipation and the Rise of the Nazis. N.p.: University of Toronto Press, Scholarly Publishing Division, 2015.

Milk Foundation. "The Official HARVEY MILK Biography." Milk Foundationorg RSS. Accessed May 24, 2021. https://milkfoundation.org/about/harvey-milk-biography/.

MPJI. "About MPJI." Marsha P. Johnson Institute. Accessed May 24, 2021. https://marshap.org/about-mpji/.

NCES. "National Assessment of Adult Literacy (NAAL)." National Center for Education Statistics (NCES) Home Page, a part of the US Department of Education. Accessed May 24, 2021. https://nces.ed.gov/naal/lit_history.asp.

Onion, Amanda, Missy Sullivan, and Matt Mullen. "Hitler Purges Members of His Own Nazi Party in Night of the Long Knives." History.com. A&E Television Networks, February 9, 2010. https://www.history.com/this-day-in-history/night-of-the-long-knives.

Pruitt, Sarah. "What Happened at the Stonewall Riots? A Timeline of the 1969 Uprising." History.com. A&E Television Networks, June 13, 2019. https://www.history.com/news/stonewall-riots-timeline.

Rothberg, Emma. "Sylvia Rivera." National Women's History Museum. 2021. www.womenshistory.org/education-resources/biographies/Sylvia-Rivera.

Schillace, Brandy. "The Forgotten History of the World's First Trans Clinic." Scientific American. Scientific American, May 10, 2021. https://www.scientificamerican.com/article/the-forgotten-history-of-the-worlds-first-trans-clinic/.

Sibalis, Michael. "Homophobia, Vichy France, and the "Crime of Homosexuality": The Origins of the Ordinance of 6 August 1942." GLQ: A Journal of Lesbian and Gay Studies 8, no. 3 (2002): 301-318. muse.jhu.edu/article/12215.

Sulzenbacher, Hannes. "'Homosexual' Men in Vienna, 1938." Chapter. In Opposing Fascism: Community, Authority and

Resistance in Europe, edited by Tim Kirk and Anthony McElligott, 150–62. Cambridge: Cambridge University Press, 1999. doi:10.1017/CBO9780511497070.011.

United States Holocaust Memorial Museum. "PERSECUTION OF HOMOSEXUALS IN THE THIRD REICH." United States Holocaust Memorial Museum. United States Holocaust Memorial Museum. Accessed May 24, 2021. https://encyclopedia. ushmm.org/content/en/article/persecution-of-homosexuals-in-the-third-reich.

Waxman, Olvia B., and Joey Lautrup. "How Did the Stonewall Riots Start? Even Experts Don't Agree." Time. Time, May 31, 2019. https://time.com/5598363/stonewall-beginnings-history/.

Wills, Matthew. "Ernst Röhm, The Highest-Ranking Gay Nazi." JSTOR Daily. JSTOR, March 27, 2017. https://daily.jstor.org/ernst-rohm-the-highest-ranking-gay-nazi/.

Yardley, William. "Storme DeLarverie, Early Leader in the Gay Rights Movement, Dies at 93." The New York Times. The New York Times, May 29, 2014. https://www.nytimes.com/2014/05/30/nyregion/storme-delarverie-early-leader-in-the-gay-rights-movement-dies-at-93.html.

CHAPTER 4: THE AIDS PANDEMIC

"A Timeline of HIV and AIDS." HIV.gov, April 8, 2021. https://www.hiv.gov/hiv-basics/overview/history/hiv-and-aids-timeline.

Aizenman, Nurith. "How To Demand A Medical Breakthrough: Lessons From The AIDS Fight." NPR. NPR,

February 9, 2019. https://www.npr.org/sections/health-shots/2019/02/09/689924838/how-to-demand-a-medical-breakthrough-lessons-from-the-aids-fight.

Altman, Lawrence K. "New Homosexual Disorder Worries Health Officials." The New York Times. The New York Times, May 11, 1982. https://www.nytimes.com/1982/05/11/science/new-homosexual-disorder-worries-health-officials.html.

"History." GMHC, October 23, 2020. https://www.gmhc.org/history/.

Kennedy, Mark. "Larry Kramer, Playwright and AIDS Activist, Dies at 84." AP NEWS. Associated Press, May 27, 2020. https://apnews.com/article/9525f22e3d9c78fc46378a060bf40f36.

Lopez, German. "The Reagan Administration's Unbelievable Response to the HIV/AIDS Epidemic." Vox. Vox, December 1, 2015. https://www.vox.com/2015/12/1/9828348/ronald-reagan-hiv-aids.

Pear, Robert. "Health Chief Calls ADIS Battle 'No. 1 Priority'." The New York Times. The New York Times, May 25, 1983. https://www.nytimes.com/1983/05/25/us/health-chief-calls-aids-battle-no-1-priority.html.

Tanne, Janice Hopkins. "On the Front Lines Against the AIDS Epidemic." New York Magazine. New York Magazine, August 12, 2008. https://nymag.com/health/features/49240/index4.html.

"The History of the Quilt ." National AIDS Memorial. Accessed May 28, 2021. https://www.aidsmemorial.org/quilt-history.

The Plague of Our Time: The HIV/AIDS Epidemic. NEJMvideo, 2012. https://www.youtube.com/watch?v=hgcQfIt1kqw.

Tanne, Janice Hopkins. "On the Front Lines Against the AIDS Epidemic." New York Magazine. New York Magazine, August 12, 2008. https://nymag.com/health/features/49240/index4.html.

CHAPTER 5: LEGALIZING RESILIENCE

Biden , Joseph R. "Executive Order on Enabling All Qualified Americans to Serve Their Country in Uniform." The White House. The United States Government, January 25, 2021. https://www.whitehouse.gov/briefing-room/presidential-actions/2021/01/25/executive-order-on-enabling-all-qualified-americans-to-serve-their-country-in-uniform/.

Bumiller, Elisabeth. "Pentagon Sees Little Risk in Allowing Gay Men and Women to Serve Openly." The New York Times. The New York Times, November 30, 2010. https://www.nytimes.com/2010/12/01/us/politics/01military.html.

Chozick, Amy. "Hillary Clinton, Loudly and Proudly, Taps Into a Vein of Support Among Gay Voters." The New York Times. The New York Times, July 1, 2015. https://www.nytimes.com/2015/07/02/us/politics/hillary-clinton-courts-gay-lgbtq-voters.html.

Hartenstein, Meena. "Bill Clinton Regrets 'Don't Ask, Don't Tell' Policy, Says It Was Meant to Protect Gay Soldiers." nydailynews.com. New York Daily News, September 21, 2010. https://www.nydailynews.com/news/politics/bill-clinton-regrets-don-don-policy-meant-protect-gay-soldiers-article-1.441841.

Honan, Edith. "Factbox: List of States That Legalized Gay Marriage
." Reuters. Thomson Reuters, June 26, 2013. https://www.reuters.
com/article/us-usa-court-gaymarriage-states/factbox-list-of-
states-that-legalized-gay-marriage-idUSBRE95P07A20130626.

H.R.3396 - 104th Congress (1995-1996): Defense of Marriage Act,
H.R.3396, 104th Cong. (1996), https://www.congress.gov/
bill/104th-congress/house-bill/3396.

HRC "Business Coalition for the Equality Act." Human Rights
Campaign. 2021. Accessed May 29, 2021. https://www.hrc.org/
resources/business-coalition-for-equality.

Kurtzleben, Danielle. "House Passes The Equality Act: Here's What
It Would Do." NPR. NPR, February 24, 2021. https://www.npr.
org/2021/02/24/969591569/house-to-vote-on-equality-act-her-
es-what-the-law-would-do.

Lee, Jesse. "The President Signs Repeal of 'Don't Ask Don't Tell':
'Out of Many, We Are One.'" The White House President
Barack Obama . National Archives and Records Administration, December 22, 2010. https://obamawhitehouse.archives.
gov/blog/2010/12/22/president-signs-repeal-dont-ask-dont-tell-
out-many-we-are-one.

Maddow, Rachel. Other. *Clinton on Undoing Her Husband's Policies.* MSNBC, October 23, 2015. https://www.msnbc.com/
rachel-maddow/watch/clinton-on-undoing-her-husbands-pol-
icies-550898243537.

MAP. "Religious Exemption Laws." Movement Advancement Project, June 14, 2021. https://www.lgbtmap.org/equality-maps/religious_exemption_laws.

Neuman, Scott. "Obama: Supreme Court Same-Sex Marriage Ruling 'A Victory For America'." NPR. NPR, June 26, 2015. https://www.npr.org/sections/thetwo-way/2015/06/26/417731614/obama-supreme-court-ruling-on-gay-marriage-a-victory-for-america.

"Obergefell v. Hodges." Oyez. Accessed May 29, 2021. https://www.oyez.org/cases/2014/14-556.

Pruitt, Sarah. "Once Banned, Then Silenced: How Clinton's 'Don't Ask, Don't Tell' Policy Affected LGBT Military." History.com. A&E Television Networks, April 25, 2018. https://www.history.com/news/dont-ask-dont-tell-repeal-compromise#:~:text=In%201993%2C%20when%20President%20Bill,cause%20problems%20within%20military%20ranks.

Ramsey, Nick. "How--and Why--DOMA Became Law in 1996." MSNBC. NBCUniversal News Group, March 30, 2013. https://www.msnbc.com/the-last-word/how-and-why-doma-became-law-1996-msna20387.

The Congressional Club Museum and Foundation, 2020. https://www.thecongressionalclubmuseumandfoundation.org/.

Thompson, Matt. "How to Spark Panic and Confusion in Three Tweets." The Atlantic. Atlantic Media Company, January 14, 2019. https://www.theatlantic.com/politics/archive/2019/01/

donald-trump-tweets-transgender-military-service-ban/579655/.

CHAPTER 6: THE SCIENCE OF RESILIENCE

Gorman, Amanda. *The Hill We Climb: an Inaugural Poem for the Country.* New York City, NY: Viking Books for Young Readers, an imprint of Penguin Random House, 2021.

Hone, Lucy. "3 Secrets of Resilient People." TED, August 2019. https://www.ted.com/talks/lucy_hone_3_secrets_of_resilient_people/up-next.

Hone, Lucy "Lucy Hone Resilience Expert and Researcher." TED Speaker. TED, 2020. https://www.ted.com/speakers/lucy_hone?language=en.

Rose, Raphael. "How Failure Cultivates Resilience." TED, November 2018. https://www.ted.com/talks/raphael_rose_how_failure_cultivates_resilience.

SAMHSA. "2019 National Survey on Drug Use and Health: Lesbian, Gay, & Bisexual (LGB) Adults: CBHSQ Data." SAMHSA.gov, September 2020. https://www.samhsa.gov/data/report/2019-nsduh-lesbian-gay-bisexual-lgb-adults.

Torres, Roselinde. "What It Takes to Be a Great Leader." TED, October 2013. https://www.ted.com/talks/roselinde_torres_what_it_takes_to_be_a_great_leader.

CHAPTER 7: LEADING WITH MERIT

Fries, Steve. "The First Openly Gay Person to Win an Election in America Was Not Harvey Milk." Bloomberg.com. Bloomberg, December 11, 2015. https://www.bloomberg.com/news/features/2015-12-11/the-first-openly-gay-person-to-win-an-election-in-america-was-not-harvey-milk.

Gianoulis, Tina. Noble, Elaine (b. 1944). glbtq, 2015. http://www.glbtqarchive.com/ssh/noble_e_S.pdf.

Ledbetter, Les. "Bill on Homosexual Rights Advances in San Francisco." The New York Times. The New York Times, March 22, 1978. https://www.nytimes.com/1978/03/22/archives/bill-on-homosexual-rights-advances-in-san-francisco.html.

Onion, Amanda, Missy Sullivan, and Matt Mullen. "Harvey Milk." History.com. A&E Television Networks, June 7, 2017. https://www.history.com/topics/gay-rights/harvey-milk.

Ring, Trudy. "The Briggs Initiative: Remembering a Crucial Moment in Gay History." ADVOCATE. Advocate.com, August 31, 2018. https://www.advocate.com/politics/2018/8/31/briggs-initiative-remembering-crucial-moment-gay-history.

Roem, Danica. "My Promise to District 13." Danica Roem House District 13. Friends of Danica Roem . Accessed June 1, 2021. https://www.delegatedanicaroem.com/our-vision.

Schlittler, Ron. "Elaine Noble." Elaine Noble - OutHistory, 2009. https://web.archive.org/web/20090609065738/http://www.outhistory.org/wiki/Elaine_Noble.

Schwamb, Don. Jim Yeadon-- Bio- People in the History of Gay & Lesbian Life, Milwaukee WI, 2007. http://www.mkelgbthist. org/people/peo-y/yeadon_jim.htm.

"The Official Harvey Milk Biography." MilkFoundation.org home of the Harvey Milk Foundation . Harvey Milk Foundation. Accessed June 1, 2021. https://milkfoundation.org/about/harvey-milk-biography/.

Totenberg, Nina. "Supreme Court Delivers Major Victory To LGBTQ Employees." NPR. NPR, June 15, 2020. https://www. npr.org/2020/06/15/863498848/supreme-court-delivers-major-victory-to-lgbtq-employees.

CHAPTER 8: LEADING FIRST AND FOREMOST

Alves, Henrique Napoleão. "Chomsky and Spider-Man: 'With Great Power There Must Also Come Great Responsibility.'" Medium. Medium, April 14, 2020. https://hnalves.medium. com/chomsky-and-spider-man-with-great-power-there-must-also-come-great-responsibility-6085bbb7939e.

Apple. "Apple Reports Second Quarter Results." Apple Newsroom, April 28, 2021. https://www.apple.com/newsroom/2021/04/apple-reports-second-quarter-results/.

Arthur, Charles. "Steve Jobs Steps down as Apple CEO." The Guardian. Guardian News and Media, August 24, 2011. https:// www.theguardian.com/technology/2011/aug/25/jobs-quits-apple.

Baska, Maggie, Ed Nightingale, Lily Wakefield, and Emma Powys Maurice. "Trans Pride Flag Emoji Finally Rolled out to IPhone after Years of Tireless Campaigning. Here's How to Get It." PinkNews, November 6, 2020. https://www.pinknews.co.uk/2020/11/06/trans-flag-emoji-pride-apple-iphone-ipad-ios/.

Cain, Áine. "A Look inside the Daily Routine of Apple CEO Tim Cook, Who Wakes up before Dawn and Gets up to 800 Emails a Day." Business Insider. Business Insider, November 1, 2018. https://www.businessinsider.com/tim-cook-daily-routine-apple-ceo-2017-9#next-cook-hits-the-gym-around-5-am-the-ceo-doesnt-work-out-on-apples-campus-however-he-prefers-the-privacy-of-an-outside-gym-5.

Cook , Tim. "Tim Cook Speaks Up." Bloomberg.com. Bloomberg, October 14, 2014. https://www.bloomberg.com/news/articles/2014-10-30/tim-cook-speaks-up.

Fairbanks, Hannah. "Openly LGBTQ+ Fortune 500 CEOs and Who Could Be Next." The Riveter, June 29, 2020. https://theriveter.co/voice/openly-lgbtq-fortune-500-ceos-who-will-be-next/.

Gil, Lory. "Here's Every Apple Watch Pride Edition Band since 2016." iMore. iMore, June 1, 2020. https://www.imore.com/apple-pride-apple-watch.

Markoff, John. "Apple's Visionary Redefined Digital Age." The New York Times. The New York Times, October 6, 2011. https://www.nytimes.com/2011/10/06/business/steve-jobs-of-apple-dies-at-56.html.

Nicas, Jack. "Apple Is Worth $1,000,000,000,000. Two Decades Ago, It Was Almost Bankrupt." The New York Times. The New York Times, August 2, 2018. https://www.nytimes.com/2018/08/02/technology/apple-stock-1-trillion-market-cap.html.

NikkieTutorials: Layers Of Me. YouTube. YouTube, 2020. https://www.youtube.com/watch?v=Nx1Jp2U23PM.

Stiffler, Scott. "Apple Ads Fall Far from the LGBT Tree." Washington Blade: LGBTQ News, Politics, LGBTQ Rights, Gay News, September 18, 2019. https://www.washingtonblade.com/2019/09/18/apple-ads-fall-far-from-the-lgbt-tree/.

"Tim Cook." Apple Leadership. Apple. Accessed May 29, 2021. https://www.apple.com/leadership/tim-cook/#:~:text=Before%20being%20named%20CEO%20in,in%20all%20markets%20and%20countries.

CHAPTER 9: LEADING THROUGH TRUTH, TRUST, AND PIXIE DUST

HRC. "Fatal Violence Against the Transgender and Gender Non-Conforming Community in 2021." Resources. HRC, 2020. https://www.hrc.org/resources/fatal-violence-against-the-transgender-and-gender-non-conforming-community-in-2021.

Jonathan Van Ness Talks Queer Eye, Non-Binary Identity and Self Care | Audible Sessions. Audible UK, 2019. https://www.youtube.com/watch?v=KR356JH4mSE.

Leon, Rodrigo. "Daniela Vega En La Moneda: 'En Mi Carnet Hay Un Nombre Que No Es Mi Nombre'." El Dinamo. El Dinamo, March 6, 2018. https://www.eldinamo.cl/nacional/2018/03/06/daniela-vega-en-la-moneda-en-mi-carnet-hay-un-nombre-que-no-es-mi-nombre/.

Mayor Pete Buttigieg at LGBTQ Victory Fund National Champagne Brunch 2019. Victory Fund, 2019. https://www.youtube.com/watch?v=MD9gN7e8CQY.

Press, The Associated. "Senate Confirms Pete Buttigieg as Transportation Secretary." NBCNews.com. NBCUniversal News Group, February 2, 2021. https://www.nbcnews.com/politics/congress/senate-confirms-pete-buttigieg-transportation-secretary-n1256506.

Tirado, Fran. "'Queer Eyes' Jonathan Van Ness: 'I'm Nonbinary.'" OUT. OUT, June 15, 2019. https://www.out.com/lifestyle/2019/6/10/queer-eyes-jonathan-van-ness-im-nonbinary.

CHAPTER 10: LEADING THROUGH EMPATHY

Army, Department of the. FM 6-22 Leader Development . Department of the Army, June 30, 2015. https://fas.org/irp/doddir/army/fm6-22.pdf.

Greer, Reggie. "Joe Biden Will Fight For Queer People With Disabilities Like Me." OUT. Out Magazine, October 17, 2020. https://www.out.com/commentary/2020/10/17/joe-biden-will-fight-queer-people-disabilities-me.

Merriam-Webster.com Dictionary, s.v. "empathy," accessed May 31, 2021, https://www.merriam-webster.com/dictionary/empathy.

OUT. "OUT100 2020 List." OUT, December 4, 2020. https://www.out.com/print/2020/11/19/see-he-full-2020-out100-list-here#-media-gallery-media-54.

Scissor Sisters. *Let's Have a Kiki*. CD. *Lets Have a Kiki*. Scissor Sisters, 2011.

CHAPTER 11: LEADING UNAPOLOGETICALLY

HRC. Dominique Jackson at the 23rd Annual HRC National Dinner. YouTube, October 1, 2019. https://www.youtube.com/watch?v=DhjxDgdB24U.

Mondy, Lincoln. "New YouTube Series, Kikis With Louie, Explores Social and Cultural Issues Impacting LGBTQ Youth of Color." Advocates for Youth, November 29, 2018. https://www.advocatesforyouth.org/press-releases/new-youtube-se-ries-kikis-with-louie-explores-social-and-cultural-issues-im-pacting-lgbtq-youth-of-color/.

Stansfield, Ted. "The World According to Indya Moore." Dazed, February 25, 2021. https://www.dazeddigital.com/life-culture/article/51982/1/the-world-according-to-indya-moore-interview.

Yuan, Jada. "Indya Moore Just Wants to Be Free." ELLE, May 9, 2019. https://www.elle.com/culture/movies-tv/a27378298/indya-moore-transgender-pose-interview/.

CHAPTER 12: LEADING THROUGH COMMUNITY

Avery, Dan. "Nearly Half of LGBTQ Adults Are Religious, US Study Finds." NBCNews.com. NBCUniversal News Group, November 29, 2020. https://www.nbcnews.com/feature/nbc-out/nearly-half-lgbtq-adults-are-religious-u-s-study-finds-n1249273.

Bridgers, Georgia. *Queer Faith: In Our Own Words. QUEER FAITH: In Our Own Words.* YouTube, 2020. https://www.youtube.com/watch?v=YgZdATkGyug&t=3364s.

Broverman, Neal. "LGBT Support for Trump Doubled Since 2016, Early Exit Polls Show." ADVOCATE. Advocate.com, November 4, 2020. https://www.advocate.com/election/2020/11/04/lgbt-support-trump-doubled-2016-early-exit-polls-show.

Cox, Lauren. "Meet Rev. Naomi, the New Director for Faith-Based and Interfaith Affairs: Faith-Based and Interfaith Affairs." City of Philadelphia, October 8, 2019. https://www.phila.gov/2019-10-08-meet-rev-naomi-the-new-director-for-faith-based-and-interfaith-affairs/.

Longwell, Sarah. Longwell Partners, May 17, 2021. https://www.longwellpartners.com/.

Masjid al-Rabia. Masjid al-Rabia, 2021. https://masjidalrabia.org/about-masjidalrabia.

Merriam-Webster.com Dictionary, s.v. "community," accessed June 17, 2021, https://www.merriam-webster.com/dictionary/community.

Mos-Shogbamimu, Shola, ed. "Women in Leadership Publication 2019 Winter Issue." Women In Leadership. Women in Leadership Publication, 2019. https://cloud.3dissue.com/184930/185400/216347/WomeninLeadershippublication2019WinterIssue/index.html?r=53&fbclid=IwAR05F-NohIIC-ecw8IChGwK-WH1IXboBJWNKR5V0Wbux3ozp-9W8Qy59ut1Xs.

Namir, Hasan. *God in Pink*. Arsenal Pulp Press, 2015.

Shurka, Matthew. "Conversion Therapy Bans by US State." Born Perfect. NCLR, May 12, 2020. https://bornperfect.org/facts/conversion-therapy-bans-by-state/.

Siddiqi, Maggie, Emily London, and Luke Wallis. "9 LGBTQ Faith Leaders to Watch in 2019." Center for American Progress, August 3, 2020. https://www.americanprogress.org/issues/religion/news/2019/09/09/474156/9-lgbtq-faith-leaders-watch-2019/.

VICE. Conservatives and Progressives Debate LGBTQ+ Issues in American Politics. VICE, 2019. https://video.vice.com/en_us/video/conservatives-progressives-debate-lgbtqia-issues-american-politics/5d138f0abe4077498c793d95.

CHAPTER 14: THE RAINBOW ROAD AHEAD

Census. "US and World Population Clock." Population Clock. US Census Bureau , 2021. https://www.census.gov/popclock/.

Chee, Alexander. "What Will Gay Culture Look Like in 2035?" The New Republic, June 24, 2015. https://newrepublic.com/article/122120/what-will-gay-culture-look-2035.

Jones, Jeffrey m. "LGBT Identification Rises to 5.6% in Latest US Estimate." Gallup.com. Gallup, February 24, 2021. https://news. gallup.com/poll/329708/lgbt-identification-rises-latest-estimate.aspx.

Mallory, Christy. "The 2020 LGBT Vote." Williams Institute. UCLA, October 2019. https://williamsinstitute.law.ucla.edu/ publications/the-2020-lgbt-vote/

"Map of Countries That Criminalise LGBT People." Human Dignity Trust, 2021. https://www.humandignitytrust.org/lgbt-the-law/map-of-criminalisation/?type_filter=death_pen_applies.